D1308148

THE ARCHITECT'S
BUSINESS PROBLEM SOLVER

Kevin Mason, AIA

McGraw-Hill

New York   San Francisco   Washington, D.C.   Auckland   Bogotá
Caracas   Lisbon   London   Madrid   Mexico City   Milan
Montreal   New Delhi   San Juan   Singapore
Sydney   Tokyo   Toronto

Cataloging-in-Publication Data is on file with the Library of Congress

Copyright© 2000 by The McGraw-Hill Companies. All rights reserved. Printed in the United States of America. Except as permitted under the United States Copyright Act of 1976, no part of this publication may be reproduced or distributed in any form or by any means, or stored in a data base or retrieval system, without the prior written permission of the publisher.

1 2 3 4 5 6 7 8 9 0 DOC DOC 0 9 8 7 6 5 4 3 2 1 0

P/N 0-07-136138-3

ISBN 0-07-041106-9

The sponsoring editor for this book was Wendy Lochner, the editing supervisor was Steven Melvin, and the production supervisor was Sherri Souffrance. It was designed and set in Minion by Michael Mendelsohn at MM Design 2000, Inc.

R.R. Donnelley and Sons Company, Inc., was printer and binder.

McGraw-Hill books are available at special quantity discounts to use as premiums and sales promotions, or for use in corporate training programs. For more information, please write to the Director of Special Sales, McGraw-Hill, 2 Penn Plaza, New York, NY 10121-2298. Or contact your local bookstore.

 This book is printed on recycled, acid-free paper containing a minimum of 50% recycled, de-inked fiber.

Information contained in this work has been obtained by The McGraw-Hill Companies, Inc., ("McGraw-Hill") from sources believed to be reliable. However, neither McGraw-Hill nor its authors guarantees the accuracy or completeness of any information published herein and neither McGraw-Hill nor its authors shall be responsible for any errors, omissions, or damages arising out of use of this information. This work is published with the understanding that McGraw-Hill and its authors are supplying information, but not attempting to render engineering or other professional services. If such services are required, the assistance of an appropriate professional should be sought.

CONTENTS

SECTION 1: BUILDING BLOCKS

SECTION 2: PEOPLE

SECTION 3: TIME

SECTION 5: STUFF

To my family, whose oft-repeated utterances about life over the years foretold of the subject matter of this book:

To my father, who advises:
"If you don't have problems, you're not doing anything."

To my mother, who observes:
"People create their own problems."

To my brother, who inquires:
"What's the problem?"

FOREWORD

"Your future will be built on a firm foundation."
—Chinese Fortune Cookie

When fate handed me such a fortune, I thought it fitting for an architect, especially a Mason about to set sail in his own practice for the first time. Smiling to myself as I read its sunny prediction, I pondered the threat of stormy weather ahead: How ready was I to embark on what could be the most perilous leg of my journey as an architect?

I looked to my professional resume for affirmation. It adhered to the customary format of sequentially listing educational and professional experiences, the formative influences of which purportedly contributed to my qualifications as architect. Certainly, learning "this and that" afforded me a number of useful skills, and working "here and there" gave me a variety of experiences on which to draw. Yet it was the *changing* from this *to* that and the *moving* from here *to* there that contributed more to my capabilities as an architect than any individual skill or position. In other words, *action* encouraged *advancement*.

The blank spaces between the lines of job titles and responsibilities revealed a plainer truth about my advancement from architecture major to emerging sole practitioner. Suffice it to say that gaps in my formal education, holes in my internship, and the absence of certain experiences left me susceptible to making mistakes, particularly in launching and running my own business. Naturally, friends in the field offered moral support, but their experiences differed too drastically from mine to apply to my situation. And former employers' advice proved irrelevant to the focus of my fledgling practice.

With limited human resources at my disposal, I turned to printed matter for help. I looked at magazines, trade journals, and newsletters—anything that would give me the information I needed to handle the vast array of situations in which I found myself inextricably stuck. I dusted off the collection of practice-related books I had collected fortuitously in my travels as an intern architect. I joined two architects' book clubs. I ordered books from every source imaginable to help me fill in the blanks of my education, internship, and business experience. Books took the place of colleagues. And I relied on their authors' experiences to make up for my lack thereof. What they couldn't tell me, I figured out for myself. Thus self-reliance, combined with strong research skills, not to mention a healthy sense of self-preservation, gave me the firm foundation I needed to start and run my own architecture practice.

The Architect's Business Problem Solver shares many of the lessons I've learned since opening my practice nearly a decade ago. Within these pages are the things I did or would do when faced with the problems posed throughout this book. I hope, between the lines of problems and solutions presented here, you will recognize the panic, the frustration, and the uncertainty that pour on our architecture practices and will come to agree with me that it is action that ensures protection from the precipitation that threatens practice.

INTRODUCTION

**As architects, we undergo years of arduous training,
only to find ourselves naked in the land of practice.**
—Dana Cuff
Architecture: The Story of Practice

Our tradition of beholding architecture as art while overlooking architecture as business creates an imbalance that causes architectural practice to list. Our artist's view of architecture becomes narrowly focused in the architecture school design studio, where disproportionate amounts of time invested there rob time from other courses in the curriculum, particularly the more practical ones. Arriving in the new world of practice, we cannot help but notice the glaring mismatch between our skills as architects and the skills required to participate wholly in architectural practice. At best, the opposing elements of architectural practice, design versus business, coexist with a disdainful eye toward each other. In *Architecture: The Story of Practice,* Dana Cuff (1991: 11) observes: "While practitioners recognize the inescapable link between the two, it is by no means a happy marriage." That, according to Cuff (1991: 257), it is no easy task to reconcile the two confirms what I observed in my years as an employee in architectural firms and have struggled with as principal of my own firm: ". . . At present, the proposition that good business practices can be integrated with excellent building design is greeted with a fair amount of skepticism."

The Architect's Business Problem Solver recognizes this skepticism and acknowledges our divided loyalty to both design and business. Ultimately, its goal is to help us concentrate on the architecture. While some may argue that this goal just furthers the rift between the two sides of practice, I believe that the rift can be closed by the little measures that make up this book. Further, *The Architect's Business Problem Solver* attends to the rickety bridge that already extends over the rift: the relationships among the participants in architecture projects and, therefore, practice. We can no longer ignore the importance of people in the process of architecture. Nor can we deny that it is impossible to identify participants' roles as belonging to either the practice or the projects.

Playing the role of desktop counselor, *The Architect's Business Problem Solver* attempts, in small, strategic ways, to conciliate the opposing forces of architectural practice with easy-to-use solutions to the problems that arise in day-to-day practice. Self-improvement books and their ilk, while not panaceas for life's woes, identify common foibles that make people alike. Why should individuals struggle with problems that someone else has solved before? Similarly, why should we hassle with common business dilemmas that take us away from our drafting boards?

The books that deal with starting and operating a design practice, while well worth the time to read, tend to outline a sequence of procedures, thereby implying that architectural practice follows a sequential path from here to there. Yet we all know that situations arise in practice that threaten to sink our ships. When tidal waves hit, they require tactical maneuvers to right our practices, not strategic discussions about ideal travel routes to avoid peril. Therefore, instead of writing a "how to" book, I wrote a "what now?" book for those occasions when an architect, lacking experienced colleagues at hand, needs to be told what to do and how to do it—now!

Cuff's portrayal of architecture as a field rife with complexity gives credence to a book that combats this complexity with simplicity. That different factions—educational, professional, governmental—set sail without regard for others only serves to sink the field of architecture as a whole, setting adrift those of us who are just trying to keep our heads above water. Indeed, while those with more experience, years, influence, power, credentials, and money than me chart their courses of choice through the choppy waters of architectural practice, I'm throwing these little lifesavers to my foundering colleagues to help keep them afloat.

INTRODUCTION

Defining the Audience

For whom is The Architect's Business Problem Solver written?

The Architect's Business Problem Solver is directed to all architects, especially those with few or no employees, who most likely work on residential, small commercial, and renovation projects. It is aimed at sole practitioners to compensate for the absence of skilled colleagues at hand. Indeed, anyone working as an architect could benefit from a large number of the tips, tactics, and techniques presented here. Architects working as government employees and facilities managers could benefit from many of the topics as well. Interior designers and landscape architects, because they are in design fields, could use this book, too.

DEFINING A PROBLEM

What constitutes a problem in *The Architect's Business Problem Solver*?

For the purposes of this book, a *problem* is defined as any task, any chore, any responsibility, any concern that takes you away from your drafting board. In addition, a *problem* is defined as a situation that you simply have never encountered before. From losing focus for lack of a mission statement, to losing patience with resistant clients, to losing time through mismanaged meetings, to losing money through unwieldy billing practices, to losing important documents in endless piles of paper, *The Archi-*

tect's Business Problem Solver offers advice for tackling situations that keep you from losing faith in yourself and losing face with those you serve.

LISTING CATEGORIES

Into what categories do the Problems fall?

Because the architectural practitioner, particularly the sole practitioner, wears many hats, from salesperson to secretary to strategist, keeping track of these hats is difficult without a system of organization. In my own practice, I identified five categories to which I assign all my hats and, therefore, my problems of practice. These make up the handful of sections that organize *The Architect's Business Problem Solver:*

Section 1: Building Blocks
Section 2: People
Section 3: Time
Section 4: Money
Section 5: Stuff

DESCRIBING THE PROBLEMS

What kinds of problems are solved in the five categories and why?

SECTION 1: Building Blocks covers fundamental issues relating to launching, organizing, maintaining, and assessing your practice, issues you may not have encountered as a student or an employee. I took no courses on practice as a student. And as an employee, I was rarely, if ever, made aware of the goals of the firms for which I worked. Topics such as mission statements, business plans, practice principles, and strategies for success are outlined briefly.

SECTION 2: People deals with the many participants in architectural practice, from clients to employees to consultants. The crux of *Architecture: The Story of Practice* is the argument that architecture is a social phenomenon, that to build good buildings, architects require the ability to deal with people properly. Cuff (1991: 66) explains: "... Many practitioners are not trained in the social arts of working with clients and consultants in negotiating a contract ... or working with regulatory agencies." In his exposé of architect and client relationships, *The Fountainheadache*, Andy Pressman (1995: xi) observes: "Personal and professional style may vary greatly, but the one constant in truly successful projects seems to be defined by indelibly etched architect and client relationships." Great emphasis is placed on the architect-client relationship. Architect and employee relationships are well represented, too. The section begins with assessment techniques for you to apply to yourself.

SECTION 3: Time offers strategies for ensuring that you do not rob time from your architectural projects but rather create more time for them through better time management. Cuff (1991: 91) points out: "Time management is one of the most common ailments of architectural practice." She points to, and I corroborate, bad habits that are cultivated in architecture school, where students' investment in the design studio takes precious time away from other courses in the curriculum. These habits are imported to the architecture office, where design concerns overshadow business concerns of the firm. While tolerable in the controlled environment of school, in practice, this has severe consequences in the form of gross inefficiency that wears on the architect-client relationship. Efficiency in the running of the business side of the practice allows more time for design. Handling meetings, using the telephone effectively, and planning your day effectively are typical of the topics covered.

SECTION 4: Money deals with a prosaic aspect of practice, from getting startup money to tracking yearly expenses to paying taxes. Its higher goal is to help you reckon with the fact that you are making architecture to generate money.

SECTION 5: Stuff, for lack of a more refined name, looks at handling everything from equipment to furniture to the vast piles of paper that accumulate in your office. "The paper trail well known in bureaucracies is also present in architecture, especially since liability has become a central concern among practitioners," states Cuff (1991: 185).

All the sections are divided into subsections, and in some cases, subsections are divided into sub-subsections. For example, Section 2: People contains subsection Clients and that subsection is divided into sub-subsections that pertain to specific aspects of dealing with clients.

Explaining the Format

What is the book's format?

Unlike other books on practice, *The Architect's Business Problem Solver* presents information in an easy-to-use problem and solution format. Each problem and solution is assigned a number that refers to its section and its place within that section. This system is similar to that of a building code, a method of organization familiar to architects.

Two icons contained within the body of the text of the book identify the different kinds of information being shared.

A lifesaver identifies a Problem and Solution.
A porthole calls out one of my anecdotes that relate to a particular solution.

Additional information that pertains to a particular problem and solution is contained within boxes that are identified with one of three headings:

Tip: A quick tip that I offer.
Caution: A caution to note.
Musing: A musing that I share with you.

INTRODUCTION

Offering Additional Information

Does *The Architect's Business Problem Solver* offer information besides that contained in the problems and solutions?

Besides the problems and solutions in the five sections, *The Architect's Business Problem Solver* features five appendices. Appendix A suggests books, companies, government agencies, organizations, periodicals, and Websites to consult for solutions that are not addressed in this book. Appendix B offers contact information for mail order supplies and the like. Appendix C supplies the standardized forms referred to throughout the book, which are available on the disk that accompanies this book. Appendix D lists key words, phrases, and concepts used throughout *The Architect's Business Problem Solver*. Appendix E lists mnemonic devices and step-by-step solutions contained in the book.

$\mathbb{I}$ NTRODUCTION

Deriving Information

From where does the information in *The Architect's Business Problem Solver* come?

The Architect's Business Problem Solver culls information from the variety of written sources, both in and out of architecture, to which I turn when faced with a dilemma. Because of the uneasy relationship between the design and business aspects of the typical practice, we tend to distinguish ourselves from other businesspeople. As a result of this disassociation, we tend not to seek help from sources outside architecture. *The Architect's Problem Solver* assembles information from some of these outside sources to comprise a book specifically aimed at architects, giving you access to information not always found in the literature aimed at and, for the most part, written by architects. The information presented represents the most straightforward treatment of topics among the different books to which I refer.

Second, regarding me as typical of the sole practitioner, *The Architect's Business Problem Solver* records many of the problems I faced and solved in my own practice so far. At a crossroads in my practice, I am neither a recruit nor an old salt. Able to start and then to run my own practice for nearly ten years, I foresee many problems ahead of me as I maintain my practice and attempt to grow it. *The Architect's Business Problem Solver* is not filled with textbook cases about starting and operating an architecture practice; books of this sort already exist. Rather, it is a book based on the day-to-day needs of practitioners like you and me.

ACKNOWLEDGMENTS

In writing a book about a profession to which I've aspired since I was ten years old, it seems appropriate to thank just about every person I have ever met. In some way, each and every one of them contributed a little to the way that I look at life in general and, therefore, to the way I look at life as an architect.

As I wrote this book, I remembered all the teachers, both in and out of architecture, whose commitment to their students' learning contributed to the work at hand. I especially remember my language teachers, whose dedication to their work inspired my work ethic.

My clients, among them family and friends, teach me universal lessons, many of which are shared here to illustrate that people make architecture. My extended family keeps me from taking myself too seriously, yet takes me and my work seriously enough to afford me opportunities to do good work. My friends outside architecture are an attentive audience who invite me to participate in creating their homes from time to time. My friends in architecture keep their fingers crossed that I continue to move forward without incident as I sail my course through architecture practice.

Several people stand out among those I have met along the way to becoming an architect and, more recently, on my way to becoming an author. Most of all, I am indebted to the authors, both in and out of architecture, whose books take the place of colleagues in my practice and fill in the gaps in my education and experience. I am grateful to them for sharing their insights into the many topics covered here.

I thank my editor, Wendy Lochner, at McGraw-Hill, whose impeccable timing in suggesting the topic for this book forced me to take pause to look back from where I came and to look forward to where I am going.

I thank Gerald Allen, who offered me the opportunity to apply my administrative skills to his practice in exchange for working on once-in-a-lifetime architecture projects.

Thanks go to Linda Nelson, who recently uncovered a treasure trove of projects in my own backyard, and to Karen Kramer, who helped me to visualize this project in its finished form.

I could not get my work done if it were not for Meg Paier, who afforded me the capacity to take my computer work with me, and for Soon Guan Ow and Lay Cheng Lee, who gave me the power to do my computer work more quickly and efficiently.

Laura Heim adds perspective to my life as a practitioner by recounting stories of architecture on the shores of academia. And Miguel Marczuk grounds me with the realities of building.

Ed Curtis, my once and future partner in architecture, keeps me on an even keel in both the low and high tides of sole practitionership. Alexandra Curtis offers constancy and Peter and Mark Curtis joy in my life.

Enough thanks can't be expressed to my brother, Keith Mason, who volunteered without hesitation to help bring this book to life.

Along with my brother, I am forever indebted to my father, Kevin L. Mason and my mother, Marie Mason, my first and best clients. They inspire me to do my best work on the most personal of levels, compelling me to approach all my other work with the sincerest of motives.

One person stands out among those who contributed to my life as a business owner. By her example, I attempt to approach my work with the unwavering integrity that she demonstrated on a daily basis during her tenure at John Blair & Company. Thank you, Joan Roberts.

BUILDING BLOCKS

Shuffle-Shoon and Amber-Locks
Sit together, building blocks;
Shuffle-Shoon is old and gray,
Amber-Locks a little child,
But together at their play
Age and Youth are reconciled.

> —Shuffle-Shoon and Amber-Locks
> Eugene Field

This section owes its name to the lessons we budding architects learned from our preschool building projects, basic lessons of strength and stability. While some lessons may have been learned by trial and error, others were taught to us by more experienced playmates.

Ironically, as architects, we make sure to provide our buildings with stable bases, while as businesspeople, we often fail to load the holds of our respective firms with sufficient ballast to steady the pitch and sway of the voyage that is architectural practice. Without strong foundations, buildings crumble like sand castles undermined by the rushing tides. Similarly, without stabilizing factors in place, our businesses topple like toddlers' first attempts at building with wooden blocks.

Of all the sections in the book, this one's solutions require the most planning on our part; therefore, the tips, tactics, and techniques presented here are not as immediately implemented as are many of the others in this book. This section arranges bits and pieces for us to use, first, to launch and to ferry our practices and, second, when we drop anchor for a spell, to chart the courses along which we will sail our practices. Follow it from stem to stern, and we may find that, without too many wrong turns, we have navigated our individual practices toward a mutual destination—success.

1 BEGINNING

 1.1 # Running Your Firm

Through a series of circumstances, I find myself at the helm of my own architectural practice for the first time. Can you give me some pointers for starting and running my new firm until I find the time to sit down and read one of those how-to books?

That's what this book, especially this section, is about. To begin, imagine human entities for your practice: a heart, a mind, and a soul. And then give thought to strengthening each of them.

THE THREE HUMAN ENTITIES OF YOUR PRACTICE

▼ Heart

What desires drive your practice? What do you hope to get out of running your own practice? Recognize and work toward fulfilling the heartfelt aspirations of your practice.

See 1.2   Writing a Mission Statement

▼ Mind

How can you build a business that will provide financial support as you pursue the loftier ambitions of your practice? How will you pay the bills? Demonstrate logic by setting practical goals and meeting them.

See 1.4   Designing a Road Map
See 1.5   Outlining a Business Plan

▼ Soul

How will you sleep at night? Develop a practice conscience to guide its heart and mind, thereby giving it a soul.

Reflect the strength of the three human entities of your practice in the image of your firm.

1.2 Writing a Mission Statement

What purpose does a mission statement serve, and how do I write one?

Defined in architectural terms, a *mission statement* describes the scale and scope of your practice. Think about how you might describe a project you are about to design: What are its requirements? Apply this same thought process to a mission statement for your practice. Here are ten steps to help you along.

TEN STEPS TO A MISSION STATEMENT

1. Decide whether your practice will be big or small.
2. If you decide big in step 1, think about having to loosen the reins of your business, giving up some control and delegating responsibilities to others.
3. Think about the sacrifices you are willing to make to make it big.
4. Think about being the best instead of being big.
5. If you decide small in step 1, think about not experiencing some of the benefits of big: large staff, well-appointed offices, etc.
6. Set real-life goals as they pertain to your practice. How much money do you want to make? How many hours are you willing to work to make it? How many days off do you want?
7. Once you have set goals in step 6, think about whether you can accept this lifestyle and for how long.

8. Set a realistic time frame to assess the financial expectations you set.
9. Be prepared to follow your mission statement with a business plan.
10. Compose a mission statement of a sentence or two. Read it. Is it accurate, honest, and exciting?

See 1.5   Outlining a Business Plan

Articulating Your Practice Values

How do I run my practice with integrity?

Voice your practice values. As a means to achieve the practical goals of your practice, develop its conscience. Here is an example of practice values, inspired by *Designing Your Practice* by Norman Kaderlan.

EXEMPLARY PRACTICE VALUES

▼ Integrity

Be ethical, candid, and just in all situations. Adopt a social conscience. Satisfy clients without compromising your integrity.

▼ Creativity

Explore alternatives by examining the obvious. Encourage innovation through a detailed understanding of project needs. Always be aware of the potential to do something meaningful.

▼ Dedication

Commit yourself to each and every project. Honor promises and commitments. Contribute to society.

▼ Communicativeness

Communicate frankly. Be sensitive and responsive to concerns raised by others, always striving for solutions.

▼ Positiveness

Adopt a positive attitude. Support others. Focus on the positive aspects of each project. Gain fulfillment out of doing your best.

▼ Confidence

Respect the contributions of individuals. Trust in their natural goodness. Give them the support and opportunities necessary to do their best.

▼ Collaboration

Help one another. Appreciate the contributions of team members. Invite input from them, respecting their opinions and participation. Share knowledge and experience freely.

▼ Excellence

Aspire to excellence in all endeavors. Strive to improve the quality of architecture by being creative, knowledgeable, and persistent.

▼ Wisdom

Use acquired knowledge and prior experiences to inform each new project. Know your limitations, seeking assistance when necessary.

▼ Consistency

Maintain high levels of quality and creativity by developing a consistent approach.

▼ Individuality

Encourage individuals to apply unique talents and to pursue personal interests within the framework of your practice.

▼ Efficiency

Be decisive. Admit when you reach the point of diminishing returns. Recognize the abilities and aspirations of others, matching them with tasks that are both challenging and stimulating.

▼ Aspiration

Strive toward short- and long-range goals. Make decisions with foresight. Be responsive to unforeseen opportunities.

▼ Simplicity

Develop simple solutions based on detailed understanding of project needs. Focus on making architecture by keeping the bureaucracy subservient to the project.

Designing a Road Map

How do I prepare a road map for my practice to reach the destination I seek?

Designing a road map for your practice means deciding how you will achieve the goals you set. Try the following.

THREE R'S OF ROAD MAPPING

▼ Research

Find out as much as you can about practices that are similar to the one you plan through whatever resources are available to you.

▼ Role models

Find out how the firms you admire operate by talking to professors, former employers, and other colleagues in the field.

▼ Rungs

Think of success as a ladder, its rungs dividing the increments of that success. Draw an analogy between your body and your practice. Will your arms pull you up the ladder, or will your legs push you? In other words, what are your business's strengths and weaknesses? Will you fall from a slippery rung? Or what are the threats to your climb? Is there a nearby elevator to whisk you to your destination? Or what opportunities exist for you to reach the top?

Having assessed the three R's, proceed to the fourth: 'riting. Write two or three pages to describe your road map.

1 PLANNING

1.5 Outlining a Business Plan

What are the goals of a business plan, and how do I develop one?

A *business plan* is comparable to an outline for a news article about your practice. It includes the who, what, when, where, why, and how of your business. Besides functioning as an agenda by which to run your business, it is an essential tool for approaching a bank for a loan. Here is a business plan checklist adapted from *How to Start and Operate Your Own Design Firm* by Albert W. Rubeling, Jr.

BUSINESS PLAN CHECKLIST

▼ Introduction

Company name
Address
Telephone number
Facsimile number
E-mail address
Website address
Contact person
Paragraph about company
Design expertise
Target markets

Financial requirements

Term of loan, operating line of credit, mortgage, etc.

Summary of proposed use of funds

▼ Firm's concept

One-page summary of firm with highlights

Table of contents

Forecast of the design profession and its growth potential

General markets

The competition

National and economic trends

Business goals: one year, long range

Marketing plan

Experience

Target markets

Forecasts: one month, first year, long range

▼ Firm's operation

Location and space

Staffing required

Equipment required

Business structure: sole proprietorship, partnership, corporation

List of officers

List of contracts with clients

Background of key personnel

Organizational chart

Action plan

Steps to accomplish this year's goals

Schedule outlining checkpoints throughout year

▼ Financial plan

Financial forecast

Preliminary balance sheet

Income and expense forecast statement

Cash flow forecast

Financing needs

Loans

▼ Appendix

List of references: banker, accountant, attorney, insurance agent

Personal net worth statement

Summary of business insurance coverage

Accounts receivable summary

Accounts payable summary

Legal agreements

Financial statements for company

Copy of company brochure

News articles on firm

See 1.7 Organizing Your Firm
See 1.8 Developing a Market Plan
See 2.7 Writing a Press Release
See 4.1 Launching a Practice
See 4.2 Getting Your Nest Egg Together
See 4.4 Finding Startup Money
See 4.5 Borrowing Money
See 4.6 Getting a Business Loan
See C.1 Business Plan Worksheet Form

1 PLANNING

1.6 Strategizing for Success

Are there any strategies I can use to ensure the success of my practice?

Success can be elusive. In architecture practice, it comes from identifying and meeting the needs of a client base in order to bring personal and financial reward. Try these steps for marketing your firm and managing your business to achieve success.

FIVE STEPS TO SUCCESS

1. Develop a marketing plan.
2. Determine the financial needs for operating your practice.
3. Diagram an organizational chart of your firm's participants.
4. Outline a business plan.
5. Obtain financing for your company on your terms.

See 1.5 Outlining a Business Plan
See 1.7 Organizing Your Firm
See 1.8 Developing a Marketing Plan
See 4.2 Getting Your Nest Egg Together
See 4.4 Finding Startup Money

1 PLANNING

 Organizing Your Firm

What is an organizational chart? Do I need one?

Like a bubble diagram that shows the relationships among the program spaces for a building project, an *organizational chart* illustrates the hierarchy of your firm in terms of the people who comprise it, from you at the top to the errand runner at the bottom. Putting together an organizational chart is a helpful exercise because you make individual staff members accountable for their responsibilities with written job descriptions.

1.8 # Developing a Marketing Plan

What is a marketing plan, and how do I develop one?

With a *marketing plan*, you put faces on your prospective clients. Giving thought to who they are and which of their needs you can meet will help you focus on the appropriate approach to get the desired results. Here are four steps to developing a marketing plan.

FOUR STEPS TO A MARKETING PLAN

1. Define your prospective clients: Who are they, and what do they need or want from you?
2. Propose how you will make contact with your prospective clients: Will it be through business associates, through social ties, through advertising, or through direct marketing?
3. Describe what it is about your service that will attract your prospective clients: Is it your brilliant design work, your many years of experience, or your ability to expedite a project?
4. Determine the number of projects you hope to take on, and can handle, in the next year, in the next 5 years.

1 PLANNING

Evaluating Situations

Is there any sure-fire strategy for dealing with any situation head-on?

To be sure, you will encounter a variety of situations under many circumstances in the practice of architecture. Sometimes, level-headedness and clear thinking fly out the window in times of stress. During spells of high anxiety or slow burn, use the following situation-analysis guide adapted from *The Art of Getting Your Own Sweet Way* by Philip B. Crosby.

▼ Awareness

1. Identify the situation.
2. State how you found out that the situation exists.
3. Describe is the potential effect of this matter.
4. Rate the seriousness of it.
5. Determine how much time you have to extricate yourself.

▼ Evaluation

1. Gather evidence that the situation exists.
2. Identify the specific source of this evidence.
3. Determine whether the evidence is factual.
4. List the steps that created the situation.
5. Determine whose mind you must change to resolve the problem.
6. State what that mind thinks now.
7. Decide how you will know when the situation is resolved.

▼ Action

1. Relate the key individuals to the key issues.
2. State why they believe this.
3. Determine how to separate them from this belief.
4. Select the best method to use in this separation.
5. Determine how to implement the method.
6. Once it is over, list the steps needed to ensure that it will never happen again.

1 IMAGEMAKING

1.10 Naming Your Firm

Does it matter what I name my firm?

The name of a firm speaks volumes with few words. Most of us don't give the names of our firms too much thought, especially if state architecture boards require that we operate under our surnames. Yet there are still nuances to consider.

The word *associates* after your name indicates that you do, indeed, have associates. Insert the word *and* before the word *associates* to indicate that you collaborate with colleagues who are licensed. Omit it before the word *associates* to indicate that while you do have collaborators, they are not licensed architects. Should *and* be spelled out or appear as an ampersand in the name of your firm? Does one or the other speak better about the unity among you and your associates? Creative alternatives to the term *associates*, like *group* or *atelier*, convey images of togetherness or elite artistry.

Abbreviations that follow your firm's name, such as *PC* or *Inc.*, tell the public about your firm's business structure.

Naturally, as a sole practitioner, I named my practice Kevin Mason, Architect. What you see is who you get. Yet prospective clients sometimes ask whether I am an "AIA," unaware that the abbreviation for the American Institute of Architects indicates membership in a professional organization, not my authority to

> **CAUTION**
> ▼
> Contact your state board of architects to check the requirements for naming your firm.

render services for their projects. There is a common misunderstanding that the letters *AIA* are to an architect what the letters *MD* are to a doctor. Some of my competitors capitalize on this misunderstanding, choosing the letters *AIA* over the word *architect* in the names of their firms. For my purposes, I want the name of my practice to state plainly that I am an architect. I list my membership in the AIA on my résumé and use its initials as part of my signature in correspondence.

 I am fortunate to have been born with a surname that has a natural association with building. It has been the subject of several amusing verbal exchanges with clients. My architect friend inherited a European surname that is a pejorative term in American slang. If your name, like my friend's, could become a liability in serving the public, consider changing it.

1 IMAGEMAKING

 **Creating an Image for Your Firm**

How do I position my practice against the competition?

Who are you, really? Your uniqueness sets you apart from competitors. Fully understanding this uniqueness and being able to describe it in words and to convey it in your actions will make you different from the others as well as a standout among them. Express your individuality. As architects, we acknowledge that individual design predilections are evident in our work. One way or another, we shine through our projects, no matter their scales or scopes. The same is true of your architectural practice, which takes on the personalities of you, your associates, and your staff. Your firm's personality must come across in everything that you say and do in day-to-day practice. That is your image.

THE THREE COMPONENTS OF YOUR FIRM'S IMAGE

▼ Thesis sentence

Just as you would for a college term paper, write a thesis sentence that defines your uniqueness and describes how you will demonstrate it in the practice of architecture.

▼ Slogan

Reduce your thesis sentence to a slogan or simple phrase that you can use to attract clients and collaborators to your practice.

See 1.12 Writing a Slogan

▼ Logo

Design a logo, choose a symbol, or select a drawing that graphically expresses your thesis sentence and slogan.

See 1.13 Designing a Logo

MUSING

**Your uniqueness helps you
to define your architectural niche.
Stand tall within it.**

Writing a Slogan

Should I have a slogan for my firm, and how do I write one?

TIP

▼

Remind your clients and collaborators of the essence of your practice by printing your slogan at the bottom of your letterhead.

Though not essential, a slogan captures the essence of your practice in a single phrase or sentence. Naturally, your slogan needs to strike a chord with prospective clients. If you have followed the suggestions throughout this section, you will certainly have penned some catchy phrases to describe your practice. Thus you may derive a slogan from your mission statement or the thesis sentence that you write in thinking about the image of your firm. Make sure that your slogan is timeless and that it will grow with your practice.

See 1.2   Writing a Mission Statement
See 1.11 Creating an Image for Your Firm

After practicing as a residential architect on my own for a year or so, I wrote my slogan to convey to clients that I would collaborate with, not dominate, them: Toward your unique vision of home.

Interestingly, I've noticed that since I started using my slogan, collaborators and competitors alike seem to be coming up with slogans of their own. Coincidence?

 **IMAGEMAKING**

 1.13 # Designing a Logo

Should I design a logo for my firm?

Big companies spend a lot of time, effort, and money to create universally recognized logos for their products. Architecture is a service that results in custom-designed products. How do you design a logo for a service? Unless you are renowned for a recognizable form of architecture, like a geodesic dome, or practice in an area that has a symbol to represent it, you may consider forgoing a logo. A monogram is an appropriate device to foster recognition. Be consistent in the graphic design of everything that leaves your office. Good design will not go unnoticed.

 I do not use a logo. Rather, I selected a perspective drawing of one of my projects that captures the essence of my slogan. I use a large version of it on the cover of my brochure, a smaller version of it on the cover of my design counseling flyer, and various versions of it in my advertisements. Because it fosters recognition among prospective clients as they come across it under a variety of circumstances, the drawing takes the place of a logo.

SECTION 2

People

You

Clients: Attracting Them

Clients: Signing Them

Clients: Refusing Them

Clients: Keeping Them

The starfish may look unimportant,
Lying limply on his underwater shelf.
He may look unimportant to you
But he's very interesting to himself.

It takes all kinds of people to make up a world,
All kinds of people and things.
They crawl on the earth,
They swim in the sea,
And they fly through the sky on wings.
All kinds of people and things,
And brother, I'll tell you my hunch:
Whether you like them
Or whether you don't,
You're stuck with the whole damn bunch!

> — Oscar Hammerstein II
> "All Kinds of People"
> *Pipe Dream*

Architecture practice makes it all too easy for us to hit sour notes among the complex chords we use to arrange our compositions for success. At times all thumbs, we are unnerved by dealings with the various people who participate in practice. Usually, our fumbling betrays our lack of experience with such interactions. And in an attempt to cover up our own shortcomings, we cast dim lights on others that in turn only reflect our own shortsightedness in not seeing the precisely outlined roles they can play in our practices. By focusing on these roles and the people who play them, we see our way clear to inviting others on our journey so that we may all enjoy success. With success, we become more confident at the helms of our practices.

Clients, sometimes family and friends, afford us the means to our ends. In adding employees and consultants, it's the people of practice who power our sails. Yet each time we head into this great source of power, we face reckoning with any individual's source of power, the ego. To successfully balance a combination of others' egos with our own is to learn to tack into the wind without tipping into the sea.

How we interact with the different factions of our collaborators depends on individual deportment. Decorum is difficult to describe, more so to prescribe. Yet certain tangible skills help us cope better with the interactions for which schooling, interning, and working as staff architects may not prepare us. Section 2, People, offers ways to hone these skills.

2 YOU

Evaluating Yourself as a Boss

How do I evaluate myself as a boss?

Whether you have employees or not, you are a boss. If you are a sole practitioner, boss is just one of the many hats you wear. If you have expanded your practice to the point where you require employees, the dynamic between you and them is worth a look.

In *Nobody Gets Rich Working for Somebody Else*, Roger Fritz enumerates the dos and don'ts of successful bosses. His points are adapted below to help evaluate your success as a boss. See how many of the following things apply to you.

FIFTEEN THINGS THAT SUCCESSFUL BOSSES DO

You are a successful boss if you:
1. Develop confidence among your employees.
2. Use your time wisely.
3. Work with people and toward goals, not on routine tasks.
4. Work as a team with your employees, encouraging their input in the decision-making process.
5. Delegate responsibility skillfully.
6. Think in a flexible manner, seeking an alternate approach if the first try fails.
7 Maintain enthusiasm for your work and engender it in your employees.

8. Value good preparation.
9. Strive to improve personal skills.
10. Work toward the future instead of living in the past.
11. Use persuasion with employees instead of authoritarianism.
12. Focus on the what and why of a failure instead of the who.
13. Hire competent, enthusiastic, well-motivated employees instead of tolerating hangers-on.
14. Promote employees on the basis of performance, not tenure.
15. Set realistic goals for you and your employees, not overextending yourself, your employees, or the practice.

See 1.7 Organizing Your Firm
See 2.34 Conducting a Successful Interview
See 2.38 Reviewing Employee Job Performance
See 2.39 Fostering Cooperation among Staff
See 3.1 Avoiding Repeated Mistakes
See 3.8 Evaluating Your Use of Time
See 3.9 Planning Time

2 YOU

2.2 Overcoming Writer's Block

I often have trouble beginning writing assignments. What can I do to overcome writer's block?

Getting started on a writing assignment can be daunting if you set your sights on the finished article in its entirety. Any written assignment can be broken down into several key elements.

Here are four methods for overcoming writer's block; use them individually or in combination.

FOUR METHODS FOR OVERCOMING WRITER'S BLOCK

1. Write as you design

Writing an article is like designing a building. The article's goal is like the building's purpose: What is its function? The points to be covered are like the rooms to be included. The outline is like a bubble diagram that shows how the parts relate to one another. The introduction is the concept. The conclusion explains how it all fits together. Begin your rough draft for an article as you would the preliminary sketches for a building.

2. Talk to yourself

If you are about to write something, think about the points you wish to make as though you are having a conversation with a friend. Thinking in terms of a spoken conversation helps you put ideas in writing when you finally sit down with pen and paper. If your writing assignment is the cause of intimidation, like the writing of a speech for a large audience, think of it as a conversation with someone who is not in a position to judge you. This helps to lessen the import of the task. After you have written down the contents of your "conversation," the bulk of your assignment will be complete, even if you have to rework it for the specific purpose.

3. Recall lessons from school

Everything you write—proposal, memorandum, agreement, transmittal, press release, a book—is intended to convey a message. Although each of these has its individual format, they all can be boiled down to the same essence. Remember your English teacher's instructions for writing a term paper. Write a thesis sentence that forecasts the content of your written piece. Compose an outline that lists the points you wish to cover. Expand the outline to include specific information about the points to cover. Write about the points in a few sentences. Connect your thoughts with transitional sentences. Sum it up with a conclusion.

4. Head to the computer

TIP

Use colored pens and pads to make your writing task seem less formidable.

If your head is a jumble with points you wish to cover in a written piece, head to the computer and enter them in stream-of-consciousness fashion. Once you have entered your thoughts, no matter how incongruous they seem at first, you have started and have therefore overcome writer's block. Once you have this jumble, organize it. The computer is a great tool for reluctant writers because it allows you "to cut and paste" sentences as a means to establish an order. Thus, unlike in a thesis, you can start in the middle and work outward.

Using Your Power to Influence

What power do I have to influence others?

Power means different things to different people. If you consider the synonyms to power—control, authority, influence, force—you will achieve a greater understanding of the power you possess as principal of your own firm. In his excellent how-to guide, *Designing Your Practice*, Norman Kaderlan explains the sources of power you might harness to run your firm. Understanding the concept of power might help you better understand your unique role at the helm of your practice. Although Kaderlan's account of power is worth reading in its entirety, a synopsis of it is presented below in an annotated outline form.

THE TWO FORMS OF A PRINCIPAL'S POWER

▼ Position power

Position power is actual power that is inexorably attached to your rank as the principal of your own firm. This form of power comes from three sources.

1. Legitimate power
This is the authority you derive from your role as principal. It manifests itself in your right to hire and fire employees, for instance.

2. Reward power

This comes from your ability to acknowledge the performance of others. An example is promoting an employee.

3. Coercive power

This is engendered by your employees' fear that you might demote or terminate them.

▼ Personal Power

Personal power is bestowed on you by the people you seek to influence. It is more of a perceptual power because it comes from other people's regard for you and your abilities. There are three sources for it as well.

1. Referent power

This comes from the way other people identify with you. It is the common bond between you and your employees, clients, etc.

2. Information power

This comes from other people's perception that you are privy to information that is not available to them.

3. Expert power

This results from the number of your skills, the vastness of your knowledge, or the degree of your expertise.

To use obvious analogies, corporate practices tend to rely on position power whereas design-oriented practices usually favor personal power.

Playing Principal

What roles should I be playing as the principal of a design firm?

The roles you play as a principal are fundamental to the management of your firm. As principal of an architecture firm, you wear many hats. As a sole practitioner, you wear even more. Norman Kaderlan, in *Designing Your Practice*, defines the eleven roles of a principal within four critical areas: interpersonal relationships, informational responsibilities, decision-making capacities, and expert capabilities. The annotated outline below presents the gist of Kaderlan's definitions.

ELEVEN ROLES TO PLAY AS PRINCIPAL

Here are 11 roles in four categories that you play as the principal of your own firm.

▼ Interpersonal relationships

1. Figurehead
Represent the practice in highly visible and symbolically important activities.

2. Leader
Accept responsibility for all the work of your firm.

3. Liaison
Communicate the goals of your practice to the outside world.

▼ Informational responsibilities

4. Monitor
Collect information from within and without your firm to keep up with emerging trends.

5. Disseminator
Distribute information to your staff that you collect in your role as monitor and believe to be useful in your role as leader.

6. Spokesperson
Share information with the outside world that you collect in your role as monitor and believe to be useful in your role as liaison.

▼ Decision-making capacities

7. Entrepreneur
Seek new courses along which to move and expand your practice.

8. Disturbance handler
Take care of unexpected interruptions in all areas of your practice.

9. Resource allocator
Decide who will get available time, money, and equipment in the day-to-day running of your practice.

10. Negotiator
Work out contracts with clients, consultants, etc., and determine salaries, benefits, etc., for your staff.

▼ Expert capabilities

11. Expert
Develop expertise in all aspects of your practice.

See 2.5 Playing Manager

Playing Manager

How can I become an effective manager?

In *Designing Your Practice*, Norman Kaderlan defines four roles for you to play as manager of your firm: producer, administrator, entrepreneur, and integrator. Both complementary and contradictory, these roles require you, or anyone else functioning in these roles, to look at your practice from several different perspectives. Functioning as an integrator helps you to balance the roles that can cause your practice to list if you favor one over the other because of your comfort in it. Here are the four roles and their functions.

FOUR ROLES TO PLAY AS MANAGER

The four roles to play as manager are:

1. Producer
Actively participate in the architecture projects of your office.

2. Administrator
Ensure that goals, both long and short term, are met for both the architectural projects and the business aspects of your practice.

3. Entrepreneur
Look for new opportunities for your practice.

---

4. Integrator

Link your roles as producer, administrator, and entrepreneur with special emphasis on relating to the people involved in the making of architecture.

See 2.4   Playing Principal

2 CLIENTS:
ATTRACTING THEM

2.6 Defining a Press Release

What is a press release?

A *press release* is a factual statement that you issue to a publication, most likely a newspaper, to announce an event or occurrence of interest to its readership. Are you establishing a residential architectural practice in your hometown? Did your firm win an award for a hospital it designed? Did you write a book about office design? Such events or occurrences are appropriate material for press releases.

TIP

It is an unspoken understanding that newspapers are more apt to print press releases of paying advertisers.

Press releases garner attention for you and your practice with the intent to elevate your stature in the eyes of your client base and, ultimately, to get more work. Orchestrating a series of press releases keeps your name before the public. Used in conjunction with advertisements, press releases help paint a clearer picture of you and your practice, beyond what ads alone can do. Contracting for a series of advertisements and backing them up with a few well-placed press releases helps to build name recognition among your client base. On the local level, it does not take much for an event or occurrence to be deemed newsworthy by newspapers.

 I released the same press release to several local newspapers to announce the offering of design counseling services, considered newsworthy because it spoke about a service of potential interest to the newspapers' readerships. Announcing design counseling services set me apart from other residential architects in my area who are not available on a limited hourly basis.

Writing a Press Release

2.7

How do I write a press release to attract attention to my practice?

A press release delivers the facts about an event or occurrence to the editor of a publication who uses them to write a news article or, in the case of small newspapers, prints them verbatim. Unlike other written pieces that build toward a conclusion, press releases are written in the form of an inverted triangle: Information is presented in the order of most to least important to allow editors to shorten articles from the bottom up. This order also allows readers to glean critical information without having to read the entire article. Below is a two-part formula for writing a press release adapted from *How To Make Yourself (or Anyone Else) Famous,* by Gloria Michels:

TWO-PART FORMULA FOR WRITING A PRESS RELEASE

▼ Part 1

Include the following contents in a press release:

Parameters In preparing a press release, follow these steps:

1. Fill a press release with essential information only, limiting yourself to one page, if possible.
2. Include contact information, listing day and evening telephone numbers.
3. Write a headline that explains the topic of the press release.

4. Use simple words to tell the facts about the event or occurrence.
5. Use quotes for subjective statements about the topic.

Body In writing a press release, answer the following four questions in the lead paragraph:

6. Who was or will be involved in the event or occurrence?
7. What happened or will happen to warrant the issuance of a press release?
8. When did or will the event or occurrence happen?
9. Where did or will the event or occurrence happen?

If it is important to the story, answer the following question in the lead paragraph:

10. Why and/or how did or will the event or occurrence happen?

Expand on the answers to the preceding questions in the rest of the press release, remembering to present the least important facts last.

▼ Part 2

The mechanics of a press release are as follows:

Format Use this format when submitting a press release:

1. Use one side of white $8^1/_2 \times 11$ inch paper or letterhead.
2. Set extrawide margins.
3. Type, word process, or computer generate double-spaced text.

Paragraphs Follow these conventions in structuring paragraphs:

4. Avoid hyphenated words at the ends of sentences.
5. Avoid breaking up individuals' titles at the ends of sentences.
6. Avoid breaking paragraphs between pages.

Conventions Use these conventions in submitting a press release:

7. Write the time of release in the upper left corner of page 1, for example:

FOR IMMEDIATE RELEASE or
FOR RELEASE AFTER MONDAY, JANUARY 1, 2005

8. To continue from another page, label the bottom center of the page:

-MORE-

9. To continue onto another page, write the title of the release in the upper left-hand corner of the page with the number of the page to be added, for example:

- add one, - add two

10. Indicate the end of the press release by writing one of the following on the bottom center of the last page:

-30-, ###, -END-

Delivery Deliver a press release using the following techniques:

11. Address the press release using the term *editor* and the particular department, not the actual editor's name if there is a chance that editors work in shifts.

12. If using a business-size envelope, French-fold the press release so that its top faces out for the editor to see on opening the envelope, or use a 9 × 12 inch envelope and do not fold the press release at all.

See 2.2   Overcoming Writer's Block

2 CLIENTS: ATTRACTING THEM

 **2.8** **Deciding Whether to Advertise**

How do I decide whether or not to advertise?

Architects are reluctant to advertise because it seems like a plea for work. Deep down, we hope that our good names and competent works bring more projects our way. Indeed, a referral is the best way to get new work because it is a recommendation.

MUSING

If the American Institute of Architects finds it beneficial to advertise, perhaps we, as individuals, can benefit from advertising, too.

Once you build a reputation and can rely on word of mouth to send new clients your way, you may decide not to advertise. However, if you are just starting out in your newly opened practice or simply want to take on more work, you need to make potential clients aware of your existence. There is no shame in advertising. Consider it one component of a larger public relations campaign designed to paint a picture of you and your practice.

An advertisement, despite a catchy slogan or attractive graphics, merely states contact information. In conjunction with press releases about you and your accomplishments, advertisements establish name recognition among your client base. Beware, advertisements open you up to inquiries from all kinds of people. Fielding these inquiries and deciding which opportunities to pursue can become a part-time job in itself.

Advertisements do not come cheap. The cost for small ads in a weekly local newspaper can eat quickly into your cash. Prepare an advertising budget and stick to it. Be frugal at first; you can always take out more advertising.

See 1.12 Writing a Slogan
See 1.13 Designing a Logo

Many of my residential architecture clients tell me how difficult it is to find an architect for their residential projects. Architects, they say, are not part of their social circle. To make matters worse, architects in the residential area compete with contractors and tradespeople who are more than willing to provide "design services." To me, advertising is not a plea for work. Rather, it is an announcement to homeowners that I am available to help them with their residential projects.

2.9 Deciding Where to Advertise

I have decided to advertise. Where do I advertise to get new clients?

Deciding where to advertise depends on the audience you are trying to reach. First, advertise in a medium that is read by your potential clients. Second, decide where to advertise by determining the geographic scope of your practice.

Do you specialize in a particular type of architecture that makes you invaluable to any project in which your expertise is sought anywhere in the country? If so, let prospective clients know about your practice on a national scale. Are you an architect who specializes in residential additions? If so, consider limiting advertisements to your geographic area.

Do you limit your practice to surrounding towns, to the state in which you run your practice, or to a region of the country? Demand for your services will help you determine the answer to this question. Also, time constraints will help you determine how far to travel for a project. Start locally and increase your geographic range as your reputation grows.

Consider the shelf life of the publication in which you advertise. A monthly magazine may be kept around and referred to time and again over the course of a month or longer by its reader, who may come across your ad several times. Daily and weekly newspapers tend to be recycled quickly. How many ads would you need to purchase in those newspapers for potential clients to come across your name over and over again?

Think about where to advertise so that your firm's name keeps appearing in front of potential clients. This engenders name recognition. Consider advertising in smaller periodicals that may have a loyal following:

◆ A community newsletter
◆ A professional organization's newsletter
◆ A theater or musical performance program

See 4.1 Launching a Practice

Fortunately, a former client offered to help me run my first public relations campaign. Familiar with the local publications, their editors and rates, and a satisfied client herself, she guided me toward publications whose advertisements would bring me more clients like her. We ran a modest ad campaign with a series of advertisements in local newspapers that were supported by press releases about my services, my accomplishments, and my achievements as a residential architect. Perhaps you can find a freelance public relations person to help you jump-start your practice.

CLIENTS:
ATTRACTING THEM

2.10 Embellishing Your Yellow Pages Listing

What are the benefits to embellishing my free Yellow Pages listing for an additional fee every month?

Although most architects probably prefer to work on a referral basis, a listing in the Yellow Pages of your local telephone book legitimizes your business and helps prospective clients find you more easily if they hear good things about your firm in passing. When you are designing your Yellow Pages listing, your sales representative will offer you several options, for which you pay extra. Consider these:

◆ Opt for a bold-print listing to stand out among plain-face listings.

◆ Add a line or two to your standard listing to call attention to a service that distinguishes you from other architects, for example, design counseling.

◆ Ask your telephone sales representative about special rates for different types of listings.

See 4.8   Offering Design Counseling Services
See 4.13   Opting for a Business Telephone Line
See 4.15   Listing in the Yellow Pages

CLIENTS:
ATTRACTING THEM

2.11 Getting Noticed

Besides advertising, what can I do to call attention to me and my practice?

To call attention to you and your practice, do things that keep your name in the public eye. Many of the following are potential topics for press releases.

A DOZEN WAYS TO GET NOTICED

1. Hang your shingle outside your office where passersby can see it.
2. Put up a sign in front of your projects under construction.
3. Give a lecture of interest to potential clients.
4. Teach architecture to grade schoolers.
5. Get interviewed in your area of expertise.
6. Write on areas of interest to potential clients.
7. Get your design work published.
8. Volunteer your time to a community group.
9. Win an award for your design work.
10. Sponsor a prize in a community giveaway.
11. Get appointed to a government committee.
12. Donate something.

See 2.6 Defining a Press Release

> **TIP**
>
>
>
> Keep your eyes open for calls for work in your state and national AIA newsletters.

2 CLIENTS: ATTRACTING THEM

Networking

How do I use networking to best advantage?

MUSING

▼

Success is the big fish you are after. The bigger your net, the more apt you are to haul in that prize catch.

In its worst form, networking is synonymous with opportunism: the exploiting of personal and professional ties to promote one's interests in disregard to the interests of others. In its best form, networking means engaging people in your life's work so that you positively affect their lives and they yours. Literally meaning "to fashion a net," networking is the weaving of the fabric of your life, which is made up of the people you have met, the places you have been, and the events you have experienced. To use networking to your advantage, remain open-minded about the people, places, and events that present themselves to you. You never know where help will come from.

Somewhat of a passive networker, I believe that life sends me the people I need at the time when I need them. I have had to learn to recognize this. Many of the people who have helped me are those I helped first, often in my capacity as an architect. Here is one example of a chain of links that help make up my net:

SIX LINKS IN MY NET

1. A neighbor recommends a carpenter to install crown moldings in my living room.

2. The carpenter becomes a general contractor who recommends me to a prospective client.
3. The prospective client becomes an actual client.
4. The actual client, who has a degree in public relations, runs my first public relations campaign.
5. The public relations campaign garners me attention among prospective clients in a historic district in which I would like to do work.
6. I begin to get commissions for projects within that historic district.

2 CLIENTS: ATTRACTING THEM

2.13 # Picking Clients

I spend a lot of time working so that prospective clients choose me over my competitors. Yet shouldn't I be giving thought to the types of clients I need to be working with to accomplish the goals I set for myself and my practice?

Good clients understand and respect the multifaceted role you play in their projects. From your initial contact with prospective clients through the design and building process, define and refine your role as architect.

The questions listed below are offered to help you elicit vital information from prospective clients. Falling into five categories identified by the acronym *PETER*, the questions will help you begin building a rock-solid relationship with prospective clients.

PETER POINTS FOR PICKING CLIENTS

In your initial conversations with prospective clients, try to answer the following questions. Many of the answers can be elicited in casual conversation, provided you direct it with care.

▼ P is for personality

◆ How do your prospective clients react to you during your initial conversations and during subsequent contact?

◆ How demanding do they seem?

- Can you communicate freely and clearly with them, or do there seem to be misunderstandings early on in your discussions?

▼ E is for experience

- Have your prospective clients worked with an architect before?
- Why are they not working with that architect now?
- How do they characterize their experience with the other architect?
- What services did that architect provide?
- Have your prospective clients ever built before? What project? How did it go?

▼ T is for timing

- Are your clients aware of and comfortable with the time frame you set for their project?
- Can you conform to your clients' timeframe without disappointing them?

▼ E is for expectations

- Why did your prospective clients contact you?
- What do they know about your design work?
- What do they know about your service?
- What do they hope to gain by working with you?

▼ R is for reserve

- Do your clients have the wherewithal, both personally and financially, to accomplish their project?
- From where will the money to fund the project come?

See 1.8 Developing a Marketing Plan
See C.2 Prospective Client Interview Notes Form

MUSING

You are already ahead of the game if clients recognize that they need an architect for their projects.

I sent a proposal to a prospective client that was similar in format and content to others that had gotten me work. I thought it was organized, straightforward, and thorough, as well as inventive and creative in its suggestions for the design of the residential addition under consideration. I learned through a mutual acquaintance that my prospective client took issue with my carefully crafted proposal, concluding from its tone that I did not want to work with him. His mistaken conclusion was the first warning sign in what became an uncomfortable working relationship on a project that, ultimately, was abandoned. I have learned to look for warning signs in early conversations with prospective clients. Ignoring such signs has led me to stormy working relationships that have only gotten worse, not better. Now I ask myself: Is the prospective outcome of the project worth the time and effort to invest in a difficult relationship with the client?

MUSING

If fate is kind,
it will send you your
worst clients first.

Deciding to Take on a Project

In the first few years of my practice, I put a lot of effort into drumming up business. I took on as many projects as I could, thinking the more the merrier. I never gave much thought to the effect of these projects on the larger goals of my practice. And looking back, I probably should have passed on several projects for one reason or another. When considering a prospective project, what do I ask myself to determine whether it suits me and my practice?

Only you can decide what makes a project good for you and your practice. In making the decision whether or not to take on any project, consider the eight reasons outlined below.

EIGHT REASONS TO TAKE ON A PROJECT

Do any of the following statements apply to the project you are considering? If so, how many? Alone, each statement below is reason enough to take on a project, yet several in combination certainly indicate a project worth taking.

1. Design
The project allows you to display your design talents.

2. Learning
The project is a first for you in terms of building type, construction techniques, or special circumstances that surround it,

providing you the opportunity to learn something important by participating in it.

3. Money
The project pays well, helping you to sustain your practice and perhaps to subsidize less well-paying projects.

4. Series
The project is the first in what may become a series of projects for a particular client.

5. Service
The project allows you to provide stellar service to a client.

6. Size
The project is similar in scale and scope to your other projects, it is small enough to squeeze in, or it is the big one you've been waiting for.

7. Timing
The project has a schedule that fits in nicely with your other projects.

8. Visibility
The project may gain you recognition in your community by its presence or may gain you recognition on a broader scale if it gets published.

See 1.8 Developing a Marketing Plan
See 2.13 Picking Clients
See 2.20 Turning Down Work

2 CLIENTS: SIGNING THEM

2.15 # Writing a Proposal

What topics do I discuss in a written proposal in order for it to be thorough?

A written proposal continues the dialogue you have established with prospective clients in your initial telephone conversations and meetings. In a written proposal, state your understanding of your clients' requirements for their project. Convince them of the benefit of your prospective contribution to it. Naturally, any proposal reflects the image of your firm and is shaped by the particular area of architecture in which you specialize. Use the following outline to write a typical proposal.

SIX SECTIONS IN A TYPICAL PROPOSAL TO CLIENTS

1. Introduction
- ◆ Thanks clients for the opportunity to submit the proposal
- ◆ Expresses your interest in the project for various reasons

2. Goals in writing proposal
- ◆ Continues the dialogue with prospective clients
- ◆ Suggests defining the terms of a prospective collaboration

3. Organization of proposal
- ◆ States how the proposal is organized
- ◆ Explains briefly the logic behind the organization

4. Discussion of the project

◆ Puts forth the background of the project, the reasons it is being undertaken as you understand them

◆ Outlines the requirements for the project as defined by the clients and clarified by you

◆ Delivers your assessment of the background of and requirements for the project

◆ Offers a particular or unique approach to the project

◆ Establishes a target construction budget for the project

◆ Sets forth fees for your participation

◆ Suggests a possible building schedule for the project

5. Related issues

◆ Discusses preliminary work to be completed for the project

◆ Discusses the form of the agreement between you and the owner

◆ Discusses your schedule for delivering services

◆ Lists selected projects and contact information for clients, general contractors, tradespeople, etc.

6. Conclusion

◆ Summarizes the goals for the project

◆ Restates your prospective contribution to the project

◆ Reiterates your interest in the project

◆ States whose turn it is to do what

See 2.2   Overcoming Writer's Block

TIP

▼

Use subheadings in your proposals to make them easier to read.

2 CLIENTS: SIGNING THEM

Testing the Waters with an Agreement

How do I set up an agreement with clients with whom I am leery about working?

What is it about the clients that makes you leery? Do you suspect that they may not be responsive to your designs? Are you worried that they may hold you responsible for aspects of the project that are out of your control, such as the construction budget and building schedule? Are your clients exhibiting inexperience, frugality, or impatience? If worries like these plague you at this early stage, you are entitled to be leery. So test the waters.

Consider entering into an agreement for only the first phase of a project, such as the schematic design phase. Such an arrangement allows you to assess how clients react to matters of design, money, and time. It gives you the opportunity to forge a relationship within a defined context. At the end of the first phase, you and your clients will be in the midst of a pause, during which you must decide whether to move forward on the project or to part company.

If you remain leery about moving forward, consider wording your agreements such that they make termination by you or your clients an option at any time. Although AIA agreements define the owner's responsibilities and allude to nonperformance of such duties as a legitimate reason for termination of an agreement, little is said about the important issue of a personality conflict between you and your client.

See 2.13 Picking Clients
See 2.14 Deciding to Take on a Project

CAUTION

Writing agreements that are easy to terminate makes the fate of projects susceptible to the whims of you and your clients.

2.17 Getting to an Agreement

Is there a strategy for getting to the point of negotiating terms with a prospective client?

Several of the tips, tactics, and techniques described in this book are aimed at getting you to the point of negotiating terms with a prospective client. Use the RPM method to move toward an agreement.

RPMs TOWARD AN AGREEMENT

▼ R

- Respond to a call from prospective clients by getting in touch with them as soon as you can.
- Relate to your prospective clients by demonstrating your understanding of their needs.
- Relay information to bolster their confidence in you as the right architect for the job by dropping a line, sending a photograph of one of your projects, or mailing your brochure.

▼ P

- Prepare for your first meeting with an agenda to establish your competence as a businessperson.
- Paint a picture of yourself as a competent designer by reviewing your past and current work.
- Present a letter of introduction that explains your method of working and the fees associated with it.

▼ **M**

- Match your clients' needs with a unique design approach in the thoughtful proposal you submit.
- Modify your approach, terms, or conditions to demonstrate your spirit of cooperation in collaboration.
- Motivate your clients to continue the dialogue you have established by encouraging contact throughout this process.

Negotiating an Agreement

I am very close to signing on another client. How do I negotiate an agreement with a prospective client?

In negotiating an agreement, work to come to terms that meet your clients' needs as they define them while meeting your requirements for a good project as you define them.

Negotiating architectural services is difficult because they are not commodities like stocks, houses, or cars. How do you put a price on their worth at the outset of a project, when you really do not know exactly what they will be? There is no simple solution to this problem.

Taking into account that no two projects are exactly alike, agreements between you and your clients are at best expanded outlines that set parameters for what you and they will do throughout the course of a project. Getting to the point of setting terms for your participation in a project is the final stage of what amounts to a kind of courtship. Since you will be asked to customize your services to the particulars of projects, think about what you are willing to do and willing not to do to participate in a project. Your personal philosophy about architecture determines how you negotiate the terms for any project. Be willing to compromise on terms but never on your personal integrity or the integrity of your projects.

See 2.19 Fielding Client Objections

TIP

If clients balk about the high amount of your fees, offer to cut back on some of the services that the clients can handle themselves. This lowers your fees without cutting your pay.

2.19 Fielding Client Objections

What are the common objections clients may have to certain aspects of terms of my service, and how do I handle them?

As in the actual construction of an architectural project, there are three critical aspects to the service you render: design, time and money. At groundbreaking, you hold onto the ideal to construct a well-designed building that is on time and within budget. A similar goal applies to the service that you provide up to the moment shovel hits ground: It should be well-orchestrated, rhythmic, and financially harmonious. Yet clients may raise objections over any one of these aspects of the performance of your services.

THREE ASPECTS OF CLIENT OBJECTIONS

1. Design
Pertaining to your design process, your clients may have one of two objections:

- You are doing more than the clients want.
- You are doing less than the clients want.

Address the objections by:

- Adjusting the level of design care in any project to suit the clients' needs and desires.
- Defending the appropriateness of your approach as it relates to the time and money aspects of your service.

2. Time

Your clients may make an issue of the time it takes for you to render your services. You can overcome strict time constraints by:

◆ Working overtime to get the job done.

◆ Hiring consultants or more staff to pick up slack.

◆ Putting more staff members on the project to ease the burden of the workload.

3. Money

Your clients may complain about your fees. You can justify your rates by

◆ Comparing them with the rates of similar firms in the area.

◆ Demonstrating how your services are superior to those of competing firms in the area.

◆ Reducing the scope of your services without taking a cut in your actual rates.

See 2.18 Negotiating an Agreement

2.20 # Turning Down Work

Do I dare turn down work?

Yes. Although financial considerations always loom on the horizon when deciding whether or not to take on a project, taking on the wrong project can do you more harm than good in the long run. For example, a never-ending, low-paying project may render you unavailable for an urgent, high-paying project. Or a long-term commitment to a service-oriented commission may have you tied down when that plum design-oriented project comes along.

Develop criteria for the projects that you desire. Make sure that the ones you take on meet your criteria. Deciding which projects to take on and then juggling them with one another is a delicate balancing act that only time and experience can help you to perfect.

See 1.8   Developing a Marketing Plan
See 2.13 Picking Clients
See 2.14 Deciding to Take on a Project
See 2.16 Testing the Waters with an Agreement
See 2.18 Negotiating an Agreement
See 2.19 Fielding Client Objections
See 2.26 Dealing with Resistance in Clients

Allying Your Clients

What are the ingredients of a successful alliance between me and my clients?

In the book *Success, Your Dream and You*, Patricia J. Raskin offers a model that she uses in her workshops and seminars to teach individuals how to market themselves. Raskin states that you create a successful alliance between you and your clients when your qualities fulfill a common purpose that is inspired by their needs. This formula is dubbed the *QPN model*.

QPN MODEL

▼ Qualities

Your qualities make you unique. Your uniqueness contributes to the image of your firm.

See 1.11 Creating an Image for Your Firm

▼ Purpose

Your purpose is outlined in your mission statement. Where it meshes with your client's purpose is your common purpose.

See 1.2 Writing a Mission Statement

▼ Needs

Your client's needs are typical of those of your market niche.

See 1.8 Developing a Marketing Plan

Retaining Clients

How do I retain clients?

Retain clients by winning them over in the first place. Over time, develop your own tips, tactics, and techniques for doing so. In the meantime, keep these eight bywords in mind to win over clients and keep them.

EIGHT -ATES TO CONCILIATE

▼ Accommodate

Be considerate of your clients' needs, their schedules, their budgets, and most of all, their special interests as they relate to their projects.

▼ Anticipate

Be aware of questions and concerns that may arise with regard to any aspect of the process of designing and building architecture.

▼ Educate

Be open to opportunities to instruct your clients in the process of designing and building architecture.

▼ Mediate

Be available to represent your clients in disputes with participants involved in any of the many aspects of designing and building their projects.

▼ Participate

Be an active participant in all the various teams that work to design and build your clients' projects.

▼ Reciprocate

Be willing to adopt a give-and-take attitude, looking for opportunities for exchanges between you and your clients that may be outside the strict terms of your agreement.

▼ Relate

Be aware of similarities between you and your clients, and look for opportunities to remark on and revel in them.

▼ Ruminate

Be thinking at all times about how you can best serve your clients.

See 2.21 Allying Your Clients
See 2.23 Defining the Effective Client and Architect Relationship

Defining the Effective Client and Architect Relationship

What are the key ingredients of an effective client and architect relationship?

As in any mutually beneficial relationship, the three key ingredients of rapport, respect, and reciprocation, the 3 R's, are present in an effective client and architect relationship.

THE 3 R's OF AN EFFECTIVE CLIENT AND ARCHITECT RELATIONSHIP

▼ Rapport

You and your client connect at some level that enables you to open a continual line of two-way communication. Others may call this chemistry.

MUSING

Respect for your clients is embodied in your design for their project.

▼ Respect

You and your client respect each other, you for your client's goals and your client for your abilities.

▼ Reciprocation

You and your client each promise to do something in exchange for something in return. This is your contract with each other.

See 2.21 Allying Your Clients
See 2.22 Retaining Clients

ARCHITECTURE
WITHOUT PEOPLE

▼

No vision to dream it

No idea to conceive it

No imagination to appreciate it

No thought to plan it

No intellect to structure it

No taste to adorn it

No talent to draw it

No mind to embrace it

No means to afford it

No process to approve it

No skill to construct it

No eye to behold it

No hand to touch it

No respect to revere it

No contempt to revile it

No reason to build it

Repeating Clients

What can I do to ensure that clients will want to use my services again?

Your brilliance as a designer ensures repeat clients. Isn't that what you wanted to hear? If it were so, there would be no need for all the books written on practice.

While design is the most visible component of the service you provide, other aspects of your service help to ensure repeat clients.

Simply put, handle your clients with care.

TIP

**Telephone
to confirm meetings
with clients.**

TIP

▼

Be punctual.

2.25 Honing Listening Skills

How can I hone my listening skills as they pertain to clients?

Hearing is a sense. Listening is a skill. Be a good listener to hear what clients say so that, in turn, you can interpret what they mean. Consider whether you possess the following attributes.

TWO ATTRIBUTES OF A GOOD LISTENER

1. You listen completely.

◆ Without interrupting your clients to ask questions or complete their sentences

◆ Without analyzing your clients' words until they are fully spoken

◆ Without being preoccupied with thoughts of matters not at hand

◆ Without giving in to distractions

2. You listen analytically.

◆ Determining your clients' intent as well as the content of their words

◆ Looking for physical behavior that contradicts your clients' words

◆ Gaining insight into your clients' personalities by listening to anecdotes

◆ Identifying confusing statements by your clients so that you can ask them to clarify them after they are done speaking

Dealing with Resistance in Clients

How do I recognize and deal with resistance in clients?

The phenomenon of resistance in clients generally manifests itself during the emotion-laden design and building phases of an architectural project. However, the first sign of resistance can appear in initial talks with prospective clients. Overcoming it is the key to reaching an agreement with them. Fear, vulnerability, mistrust, and insecurity disguise themselves in the form of resistance. This resistance can manifest itself in two ways, revealing itself in your clients' attachment to or detachment from aspects of your service that need to be discussed or resolved. Some tell-tale signs of resistance, along with responses to help you overcome it, are pointed out below.

FACING THE TWO FACES OF RESISTANCE IN CLIENTS

▼ Attachment

Your clients constantly ask you for more and more details about an aspect of your service, to which you respond that you will reveal details as they become vital to the discussion.

Your clients bombard you with too many details about an aspect of your service, to which you respond with a request for them to summarize their thoughts and to hold onto details until they become vital to the discussion.

Your clients attack you personally about issues surrounding an aspect of your service, to which you respond by acknowledging their anger and inquiring about its source.

▼ Detachment

Your clients seem too busy to deal with an aspect of your service, to which you respond by asking them for a specific time that you can discuss their project.

Your clients seem confused after you have explained an issue several times, to which you respond by asking them to articulate the nature of their confusion so that you can cover it point by point.

Your clients seem reluctant to challenge aspects of your service or to offer details of their requirements, to which you respond by commenting on their silence and opening up a discussion of their feedback.

Maintaining Momentum

How do I maintain contact with prospective clients who are considering my services and with current clients who have retained my services if I am saddled with a multitude of other tasks and responsibilities?

As you practice, you will devise ways to maintain momentum in projects by identifying mileposts to pass during the course of projects.

WAYS TO MAINTAIN MOMENTUM IN A PROJECT

▼ Thank-you note

Within a week or two after your initial meeting with clients, send a note thanking them for considering you for their project. Both courteous and clever, such a note seems like an immediate response to your prospective clients' project and buys you a little time to put together a written proposal.

▼ Telephone call

On mailing your written proposal to your prospective clients, call them to let them know that it is coming and to outline briefly its contents so that they know what to expect.

▼ Follow-up call

Within a week or so of mailing a written proposal to your prospective clients, telephone them to make sure they have received it and to inquire whether they have any immediate questions about it.

▼ Additional information

If prospective clients do not respond to your proposal within a reasonable amount of time, consider sending additional information in the form of a photograph of a similar project or a copy of one of your projects. This helps you keep in touch with them and may spur some sort of response from them.

▼ Progress report

During the course of a project, telephone your clients or write memoranda to apprise them of your progress on their projects, even if this progress has not manifested itself in the form of drawings. Keeping in touch with clients appeases them. Talk may be cheap, but it does buy time.

 When I started out in practice, I made the mistake of not keeping my clients up to date on the progress I was making on their projects. Although I spoke with them from time to time, I did not reveal any specifics about the nature of the design I was working on. Instead, I kept my ideas to myself, waiting to unveil them dramatically at the meeting to present my designs.

Looking back, I realize that my approach was formulated in the architecture school design studio, where I presented design schemes to juries only two or three times a semester. To me, it was the semester-end review, when I revealed my completed design scheme, that really mattered.

This approach does not translate well to the world of practice. Unfortunately, it took me a while to figure out that saying nothing to clients about the progress of their projects gave them the impression that I was doing nothing!

A memorable lesson for maintaining a dialogue with clients was delivered one semester in the design studio as well. One of my classmates was, by my estimation, totally unprepared for a mid-semester jury review. He pinned up drawings composed of a few faintly drawn lines, making those of us who had slaved over our pages and pages of drawings look at one another in disbelief. But when our classmate began to talk, he captured the imagination of the jury by talking about his design concept and his intentions for it. This sparked a lively discussion among the jury, much to the dismay of the rest of us who had lost a lot of sleep getting our drawings done. Because he had a receptive audience, my classmate talked his way through a review!

Such a lesson is a rude awakening for those of us who rely on our drawings to speak about ourselves as architects. What can be learned from it is that clients liked to be talked to. Talk to them about what you have done, what you are doing and what you intend to do. This keeps them informed and, therefore, contented. Ultimately, you will get your opportunity to dazzle them with your drawings, exceeding their expectations of anything you have talked about so far.

CLIENTS:
HANDLING THEM

Assigning a Client Spokesperson

2.28

When working with couples, how do I establish a spokesperson for the two so that information will be discussed and disseminated to me in an orderly fashion?

Dealing with couples is difficult because their projects usually inherit the communication style of that partnership. To maintain your sanity, explain that it is essential to begin the project from a consensus of opinion.

CAUTION

When you are working with couples, there is a point where you cease being mediator, counselor, and negotiator for the two and instead become a third wheel.

 # Making Telephone Calls to Clients

Sometimes, when telephoning clients, I feel as though they are distracted from what I believe to be important issues regarding their projects. What can I do to get them to focus on their projects?

Most of the time, it is not a question of focus but a matter of timing. Since clients' livings are usually not made from the design and construction of buildings, their projects, no matter how important, represent only one aspect of their busy lives. More than likely, you are simply calling at an inconvenient time: A father may be barbecuing chicken for his hungry family; a church committee member may be struggling with a business problem of her own. Do not take distraction personally. Instead, prepare for any telephone call you are about to make.

FIVE STEPS IN MAKING TELEPHONE CALLS TO CLIENTS

Take these actions to get the results you want:
1. Jot down a mini-agenda for any telephone call you make, just as you would plan an agenda for a meeting.
2. Estimate the time it will take to discuss the topics on your agenda.

3. Keeping in mind that a telephone call is always an interruption, ask your client whether it is a convenient time to talk when you greet him or her. Briefly explain the reason for your call, and state the time it will take to discuss it.

4. If your client is agreeable, proceed with your conversation. If your client is not agreeable, establish a time or times when he or she will be available to discuss your concerns.

5. Before hanging up, reiterate the points of your conversation, regardless of which course it takes.

2 EMPLOYEES: NEEDING THEM

Determining the Need for a New Employee

My staff and I are always inundated with work. I am tempted to hire someone to pick up the slack but am worried about another salary to pay. How do I determine whether I need to hire a new employee?

Being inundated with work is not necessarily an indication that you need to hire another employee. In *The Organized Executive*, Stephanie Winston observes that the culprit behind an overwhelming workload may be internal disorganization. She recommends that you use a checklist like the one below.

CHECKLIST TO DETERMINE NEED FOR A NEW EMPLOYEE

You need to add to your staff only if all the following statements apply to you and your staff:

◆ You and your staff are well organized individually.
◆ You and your staff work at optimal efficiency.
◆ You delegate work effectively.
◆ You and your staff use office systems that are well organized.

See 2.31 Justifying a New Employee
See 3.8 Evaluating Your Use of Time
See 3.9 Planning Time

2.31 Justifying a New Employee

I have decided to increase my staff by hiring a new employee. In the back of my mind, I am having trouble justifying the added expense. Is there a method for justifying a new employee?

There are two methods for justifying a new employee: qualitative and quantitative. The quantitative method is discussed in Section 4: Money. The qualitative method is discussed below.

QUALITATIVE METHOD TO JUSTIFY A NEW EMPLOYEE

The qualitative method to justify a new employee is based on a simple question that you ask yourself: What could I be doing with the time I spend on tasks that I could delegate to an employee? If the answer is drumming up new business, talking to clients more often, or spending more time designing architecture, then it makes sense to hire someone to relieve you of mundane tasks.

See 2.30 Determining the Need for a New Employee
See 4.10 Affording a New Employee

2 EMPLOYEES: FINDING THEM

2.32

Finding New Employees

I am thinking about expanding my practice to include staff. How do I find new employees?

Finding new employees for your firm depends on two things: the nature of the open position and the geographic location of your practice. Regarding the latter, is your practice located in the midst of a big city, a small town, or somewhere in between? The answer to this question determines where you choose to advertise for new employees.

TIP

▼

Find and try out new talent through temporary agencies without making a long-term commitment or a costly mistake.

TIP

▼

Hire individuals on a freelance basis to test their skills without making any promises.

If your practice is located in a city like New York, where you may get projects there as well as in the outlying suburbs and weekend vacation spots, advertise in a broadly circulated newspaper like the *New York Times* to find employees who hail from any of these areas. If you practice in suburban New Jersey, where your work may be focused in towns east of the Hudson River, consider advertising in a newspaper that covers the region that you serve.

Find employees in ways other than placing advertisements in newspapers. Your strategy depends on the nature of the position you wish to fill. Here is a list of typical positions in an architecture firm that need to be filled along with ideas for filling them.

HOW TO FILL OPEN POSITIONS

CAUTION

Check into the laws that determine the taxation of freelancers' fees.

TIP

Ask your blueprinter for names of draftspersons and designers who are using his or her services to put their portfolios together.

▼ Errand runner

Since the two most important requirements of an errand runner are to be willing and able-bodied, high schoolers to retirees are potential candidates for the position. Look to family and friends, former clients, and neighborhood schools and organizations.

▼ Draftsperson

Depending on the skill level of the draftsperson you seek, ask high schools, technical schools, colleges, or graduate schools to list a position in a job bank or to post it on a bulletin board. List this position in a newspaper as well. Consider testing an individual's skills by hiring him or her through a temporary agency.

▼ Designer

Fill a position for a designer through the help-wanted section of your newspaper or by asking colleagues and consultants for names of possible candidates.

▼ Secretary

The degree of experience you require of a secretary can vary. Thus you could be in search of a recent graduate of secretarial school, an individual reentering the work force, or a consummate professional familiar with the workings of an architecture office. Each of these individuals would most likely be found through different sources. Try any of the routes explained above.

▼ Office administrator

The skills required for the position of office administrator suggest a standard approach to locating such an individual: advertise. Other avenues may provide candidates as well.

See 2.33 Writing a Job Advertisement

TIP

Local organizations run networking
workshops for the unemployed.
Look there for prospective employees.

EMPLOYEES: FINDING THEM

Writing a Job Advertisement

I have decided to hire a new employee and plan to begin my search by taking out a job advertisement. What are the elements of a good job advertisement?

Refer to the help-wanted section of your local newspaper for clues to writing a good job advertisement. Which ones stand out? Why? Which ones use a lot of words and say nothing? The goal of a good job advertisement is to entice potential candidates to put some effort into applying for the position in your firm. Be creative! Here is an outline of what a good job advertisement contains.

EIGHT PARTS OF A JOB ADVERTISEMENT

1. Description of the position
Include a brief but explicit description of the job opening that describes the position accurately.

2. Description of your firm
Include a brief description that characterizes the goals and accomplishments of your firm.

3. Description of the candidate
Include generalized qualifications of the candidate so as not to discourage applicants who would be good for your firm despite not meeting job requirements point by point.

4. Firm name (optional)

Include your firm name if its recognition factor will attract highly qualified individuals. Omit your firm name if you believe it may cause a flood of unwanted resumes.

5. Contact information

Include the reference or box number of the publication in which you are advertising, or include your mailing address. Opt for a post office box address if you are concerned about candidates dropping in uninvited.

6. Telephone number (optional)

Include your telephone number if you are prepared to screen candidates by telephone and to set up appointments for interviews as applicants call. Omit your telephone number if you cannot afford to be interrupted by a barrage of calls and if you wish to review all resumes before selecting likely candidates.

7. Instructions for submissions

Include explicit requirements for resumes and submissions such as portfolios and photographs. Omit a request for salary requirements, since it may turn away prospective assets to your firm.

8. Cutoff date for submissions (optional)

Include a cutoff date for accepting resumes if you need to fill a position within a given timeframe.

TIP

When placing an advertisement for new employees, state,
"NO PHONE CALLS PLEASE," to prevent overzealous job hunters
from interrupting you with telephone calls at work.
Consider this: If a prospective employee calls
anyway, it means he or she cannot follow instructions!

Conducting a Successful Interview

I am about to begin interviewing prospective employees for the first time ever. How do I get ready to conduct a successful interview?

Conducting a successful interview requires two things: talk a little and listen a lot. If you met someone in a social situation and were looking for a way to establish common ground, what would you say? The same applies to a job interview, except that the common ground has already been established: the job opportunity in your firm. Here are the goals of a successful interview.

EIGHT GOALS OF A SUCCESSFUL INTERVIEW

1. Conduct the interview with the ultimate goal to find an individual who would be an asset to your firm, making the job requirements secondary to an individual's qualifications.
2. Begin the interview with small talk that is unrelated to the job opening in order to put the candidate at ease to speak freely and candidly.
3. Continue the interview with open-ended, objective questions aimed at fact finding, avoiding questions that put the candidate on the defensive by criticizing resume points, work experience, etc.

MUSING

The stupidest
question I was ever
asked in a job
interview:
Are you intelligent?
The stupidest thing I
ever did in a job
interview: Answer the
stupidest question.

4. Lace the interview with opportunities for the candidate to reveal gaps, shortcomings, personality flaws, etc., that may be liabilities for your firm.

5. Pace the interview with pauses so that the candidate has time to collect his or her thoughts before answering and to pose questions about issues concerning the opening.

6. Complete the interview with the selling points of the open position.

7. Conclude the interview with an indication that you are serious in your consideration of the candidate by discussing salary and a starting date.

8. Follow the interview with telephone calls to the candidate's references.

TIP

During a job interview with a
candidate, avoid sitting behind a desk,
which is a symbol of your authority.
This may intimidate the candidate.

2.35 Making an Employment Offer

I've just been through the interviewing process and have identified my first-choice candidate for the position in my firm. How do I make an employment offer?

In *Staying Small Successfully: A Guide for Architects, Engineers and Design Professionals*, Frank A. Stasiowski outlines 15 critical points in making an employment offer.

FIFTEEN POINTS TO AN EMPLOYMENT OFFER

In extending a job offer to a prospective employee, state any of the following that apply:
1. Title of the position
2. Duties and responsibilities
3. Name and title of person to whom the new employee reports
4. Office location to which the new employee is assigned
5. Base salary in terms of amount and frequency of payment
6. Overtime requirements and basis for payment
7. Terms of benefits package
8. Date by which to accept or reject job offer
9. Start date
10. Number of hours to be worked each week
11. Dates of first performance or salary reviews
12. Perks

13. Specifics of relocation package
14. Reasons why the new employee may be able to advance beyond the position being offered
15. Any or all of the preceding in writing once the offer has been extended verbally

See 2.37   Setting Job Performance Standards
See C.4   Employment Offer Checklist Form

Socializing a New Employee

When a new employee starts to work for me, I realize that there is a period of adjustment. Yet, how do I help a new employee to fit into my firm quickly and comfortably?

Helping an employee to fit into your firm is the process of socialization, as Norman Kaderlan describes in *Designing Your Practice*. For any employee, just doing the job is not enough to survive and excel in his or her position. How a job is done is vitally important as well: Is it completed with respect for the culture and customs of the firm? Use the following tactics to socialize a new employee.

SOCIALIZING A NEW EMPLOYEE

Here are some ways to socialize a new employee:

▼ Paint a picture of your firm

Paint an accurate picture of your firm during the interview so that the prospective employee's decision to sign on becomes the first act of his or her socialization.

▼ Assign a buddy from within your firm

Pair your new employee with an existing staff member, or yourself if you have no other employees, to show him or her the mechanics of the office as well as to fill him or her in on the unspoken rules of the firm.

▼ State the values of your firm

Give a copy of your practice values to a new employee so that he or she gains a perspective from which to view the operation of your firm.

See 1.3   Articulating Your Practice Values

▼ Share the stories of your firm

Recount stories of your firm's handling of sticky situations to clue the new employee in to the way things are done in and around your office.

2.37 Setting Job Performance Standards

How do I convey to employees my expectations of their performance?

You convey your expectations to employees by setting job performance standards. Similar to educational standards set by a state for public school programs, job performance standards can be used to establish an environment in which your employees can learn from you as their mentor. As opposed to a laundry list of dos and don'ts, job performance standards define the parameters within which your employees can excel.

To set job performance standards for your employees, use the same key ingredients in your outline as in a news article.

THE 5 W's AND 1 H OF JOB PERFORMANCE STANDARDS

▼ Who

The employee

▼ What

The employee's responsibilities, one by one

▼ When

The timeliness of performing the responsibilities

▼ Where

The circumstances under which responsibilities will be fulfilled

▼ Why

The goals of the responsibilities as they relate to the employee and the practice at large

▼ How

The standard of care the employee is to use in the fulfillment of responsibilities

See C.5 Job Performance Standards Outline Form

Reviewing Employee Job Performance

2.38

Now that I actually have employees, I believe that I should set up some sort of official review system so that we can sit down to discuss how they are faring. Yet, I am unfamiliar and, admittedly, uncomfortable with the procedure for reviewing employee job performance. What should I do?

The employee review can be an uncomfortable experience for you as well as your employee, especially if its sole purpose is to run down a laundry list of accomplishments and failures as a means by which to establish fair compensation. If you regard the employee review as an opportunity to discuss your employee's goals as they relate to the goals of your practice, your meeting will be focused on how collaboration is mutually beneficial to you and your employee. Remember these tips.

SIX TIPS FOR REVIEWING EMPLOYEE JOB PERFORMANCE

Assuming you have established a positive environment in which employees are given the chance to excel, keep the following in mind when you sit down to discuss an employee's job performance:

1. Assess the employee using job performance standards that you have established previously and of which you have made the employee aware.
2. Rate the employee in terms of performance, not personality, to make the review one of objectivity, not subjectivity.

TIP

▼

To place emphasis on performance for performance's sake, follow the job performance review with a separate meeting to discuss compensation.

3. Counsel the employee in areas of fault, weakness, and failure as they relate to job skills.

4. Praise the employee for the good in what he or she has accomplished, especially if there are negatives to discuss.

5. Give the employee the opportunity to comment on his or her own job performance so that the review becomes a dialogue about the process of the work.

6. Compensate the employee with a salary that is commensurate with that employee's skill level and that reflects the salary of other similar workers in the profession.

See 2.37 Setting Job Performance Standards
See 4.11 Giving Raises

CAUTION

Give honest appraisals of an employee's job performance, or you'll face terminating a poor performer with high self-esteem that you helped to raise!

Fostering Cooperation among Staff

How do I foster cooperation among my staff?

The term *cooperation* means working together. Work to establish an environment where staff members work toward the common good of the practice. Let them know that this goodness will reflect back upon them.

To foster an environment of cooperation, set aside judgment, at least in the public arena of a group effort. Place value on every employee's contribution, no matter how big or how small, how deft or how awkward. Just as you would not expect a 6-year-old to sketch with the same level of skill as a 16-year-old, you need not expect all staff members to contribute equally to a group effort in the office. Instead, expect each to contribute equivalently. Every employee sees a situation from a different perspective, allowing him or her to make a unique contribution to your officewide endeavor.

Provided you have selected your staff carefully, create an atmosphere where you all build on one another's ideas for the good of the common goal, not the elevation of any one individual.

Dealing with a Marginal Employee

How do I deal with an employee who isn't meeting expectations?

The tips for handling a marginal employee are the very same as those you use to review any employee's job performance. A marginal employee is one who is failing to meet the job performance standards that you set for your firm. Consider taking a few steps to turn your ho-hum employee into a gung-ho employee by adopting the role of mentor. Help to develop an individual who is an asset to your firm and to the profession at large.

In addition to using the tips for reviewing employee job performance, try the following.

THREE TIPS FOR DEALING WITH A MARGINAL EMPLOYEE

1. Monitor the progress of this employee more closely than your other employees.
2. Record the progress of this employee on a progress chart or another type of record.
3. Discuss the progress of this employee with him or her using the progress chart, which should be available to both of you to use as a tool of instruction.

See 2.37 Setting Job Performance Standards
See 2.38 Reviewing Employee Job Performance

Handling Rumors

TIP

▼

In cases where you cannot reveal much about an event or situation, say nothing.

I caught wind of several rumors being spread by some of my employees. How do I handle rumors?

Cure a rumor with a dose of the truth. Rumors are bred by speculators who are not fully informed about events or situations. By keeping employees informed, you protect your work environment from the spread of rumors. In instances where you cannot reveal the whole truth for proprietary reasons, reveal as much as you can, and ask employees to bear with you until you are able to fill them in completely.

2 EMPLOYEES: MANAGING THEM

Confronting Substance Abuse

How do I recognize and deal with a colleague's substance abuse?

Unfortunately, substance abuse is a reality of the topsy-turvy world in which we live. Although substance abuse can be a highly charged emotional problem, confront it objectively. Concern yourself with a colleague's job performance. If the standards of job performance that you set for your practice are not being met because of a colleague's substance abuse problem, face the facts and deal with them. Listed below are some signs of substance abuse and several ways to deal with it.

SIGNS OF SUBSTANCE ABUSE

- Changes in work habits
- Tardiness
- Absenteeism
- Abrasive behavior
- Irrational behavior
- Lethargy
- Hyperactivity
- Slurred speech

FIVE STEPS TO DEAL WITH SUBSTANCE ABUSE

<table>
<tr><td>

TIP

Send home any colleague who reports to work under the influence of alcohol or drugs. Do not let him or her drive a car.

</td><td>

1. Review your colleague's job performance using the tips outlined in this book.
2. Recall methods for dealing with a marginal employee outlined in this book.
3. Record incidents of suspicious behavior to support your review of job performance.
4. Refrain from passing judgment on your colleague.
5. Refer your colleague to a professional for help.

See 2.37 Setting Job Performance Standards
See 2.38 Reviewing Employee Job Performance
See 2.40 Dealing with a Marginal Employee

</td></tr>
</table>

2.43 Firing an Employee

What are the grounds for firing an employee, and are there any ways to mitigate this distasteful task?

Simply fire an employee who does not meet job performance standards, which are essentially the terms of employment. Unless an employee makes a colossal blunder that justifies his or her immediate dismissal, build a case for termination as outlined below.

FOUR PARTS IN BUILDING A CASE FOR FIRING AN EMPLOYEE

> **TIP**
>
>
>
> To protect office morale, ask a fired employee to leave immediately. Pay severance instead of keeping a disgruntled employee around the office.

1. Review the employee's job performance regularly.
2. Follow the steps to deal with a marginal employee.
3. Create a paper trail that charts performance and records incidents of the employee's fault, weakness, and failure.
4. Establish a warning system to notify the nonperforming employee of his or her failure to meet your standards.

If you must fire an employee, state the facts of the case to the employee in person so that he or she is absolutely clear about the causes for dismissal.

See 2.37 Setting Job Performance Standards
See 2.38 Reviewing Employee Job Performance
See 2.40 Dealing with a Marginal Employee

Hiring Consultants

I am considering retaining the services of an image consultant to do some public relations work for my fledgling firm. How do I go about finding any consultant, and how do I assess his or her qualifications?

Regardless of what kind of consultant you wish to retain, the steps to find and to interview one are pretty much the same. Here they are.

THREE STEPS TO HIRING CONSULTANTS

1. Request referrals.

Call on family, friends, colleagues, clients, and current consultants to refer individuals with whom they have dealt personally or professionally.

TIP

Ask your blueprinter for names of
prospective consultants and
collaborators who, like you,
use blueprints in their businesses.

CAUTION

Consultants offer
paid advice for you
to use at your
discretion. Keep
their roles different
and distinct from
those of employees
on the payroll.

2. Research portrayals.

Complete background checks to ensure that prospective consultants portray themselves accurately. Make sure they handle work similar to yours by talking to their references. Check that they do, indeed, have the credentials—education, experience, licensing—that they say they have.

3. Require proposals.

No matter the reason for hiring consultants, ask for written proposals that discuss the who, what, when, where, and how much of your particular requirements. Request that the proposals address the various possible outcomes that your requirements may bring about.

2 ACCOUNTANTS

 Hiring an Accountant

What should I look for in hiring the right accountant for my firm?

The right accounting firm is

▼ Local

Its staff follows banking regulations in your area, and its location is convenient enough for you to visit in person.

▼ Informed

Its staff knows your business, having served the needs of several architectural firms already.

▼ Versatile

Its staff offers both tax and business strategies, helping you to fill out paperwork as well as counseling you in building your business.

▼ Available

Its staff attends to your practice regularly because it is not over-burdened by its current workload.

The right accountant is a

▼ Principal

He or she holds a position high enough in the firm's hierarchy to be expert at his or her job.

▼ Communicator

He or she builds a good rapport with you so that you can speak candidly about advancing your practice.

▼ Teacher

He or she makes accounting understandable.

▼ Visitor

He or she visits your firm at least once a quarter to observe the goings on first hand.

▼ Problem solver

He or she answers specific questions about your business, demonstrating familiarity with the field of architecture.

See 2.44 Hiring Consultants

2.46 Handling Your Banker

Are there any tips for handling my banker so that he or she will look favorably on me and my business when I ask for a loan?

Handling your banker is similar to handling any person with whom you have a business relationship: Establish a personal relationship so that you are treated as an individual, not as a business entity. Here are some ways to establish a relationship with your banker.

FIVE WAYS TO HANDLE YOUR BANKER

1. Find common ground.

As with anyone with whom you wish to do business, look for common ground that makes you and your banker seem alike. Were you born in the same town? Did you attend the same school? Do you share the same hobby?

2. Pay attention to details.

Remember the topics of your previous conversations so that you can revisit them with your banker. Did your banker enjoy that new vacation spot? Did he recover from that flu bug? Did she locate that hard-to-find book?

3. Show interest in your banker's work.

Showing interest in your banker's work may in turn garner his or her interest in your work. How did your banker get to his or her current position? Where is your banker headed, and will he or she remember you after the promotion?

4. Play show and tell.

Invite your banker to your office to give him or her an insider's view of your practice. How can you impress your banker with the work you are doing? What evidence can you offer to differentiate your practice from others in town?

5. Give tokens of esteem.

Appropriate tokens of esteem given at just the right times demonstrate your attention to detail, like making loan payments on time. Share a book on a common hobby. Send a birthday greeting.

2 LAWYERS

Hiring a Lawyer

How do I find a good lawyer?

If you require the services of a lawyer for day-to-day legal issues—reviewing agreements, reading leases, etc.—use the techniques for hiring any consultant. However, if you need an attorney to handle a particular case, consider the following provisos.

THREE WAYS TO HANDLE A LAWYER

1. Prepare for your initial presentation to the lawyer in order to lessen his or her time learning the facts, for which he or she bills you hourly.
2. Request that his or her written proposal address your particular case, not the generalities of cases like yours.
3. Require a specific estimate of fees accrued to the conclusion of your case to make it clear that you are not a source of unlimited income for the lawyer.

See 2.44 Hiring Consultants

TIP ▼	CAUTION ▼
Ask for monthly statements of service from lawyers so that you can keep track of accruing fees.	Long-winded telephone conversations filled with idle chitchat can become expensive if your lawyer bills by the hour in 5-minute increments.

Working for Family and Friends

Once I opened my architecture practice, family and friends lined up to be among the first clients to use my services. Should I work for family and friends?

Yes and no. Working for family and friends is personally rewarding. Working for strangers is professionally rewarding.

Family and friends can get your practice off to a good start by giving you projects with which to build your architectural portfolio. Their enthusiasm and professed confidence in your abilities provide a certain sense of security as you tackle those first projects on your own. Cutting your teeth on such projects introduces you to an emotional component that is rarely as strong in projects for strangers.

Unfortunately, when you connect with people on a social or emotional level, they often fail to recognize who you are on a professional level. As funny as it sounds, while they may trust you on a personal level, they may not entirely trust you on a professional level. This mistrust is borne of familiarity. For instance, your parents may still think of you as the toddler who was building sand castles on the beach just yesterday. Friends may recall how, as a teenager, you expressed your decorating flair by painting your bedroom walls black with Day-Glo stars. Your first great challenge in working for family and friends is to get them to set aside familiarity in favor of the propriety of your professional service. Your second great challenge is not to let propriety quash the emotional root of your creativity.

The emotional component of projects for family and friends is confounded by the exchange of money for your services. What do you charge family and friends for your services? Charge family and friends the same fees you would a stranger. Or charge them enough so that it does not cause you financial hardship, and then look to your projects with family and friends for rewards on a personal level.

Working for strangers is rewarding because it gives you credence as a professional. Strangers hire you for your expertise. And when they pay you, it does not seem like the handout that a payment from family and friends does.

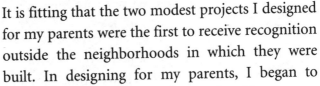 It is fitting that the two modest projects I designed for my parents were the first to receive recognition outside the neighborhoods in which they were built. In designing for my parents, I began to return the favor of their best efforts to ensure that I became an architect. Although they are among my least lucrative, projects I designed for family and friends are among my most creative and, therefore, most successful. My family and friends provided me with the proving ground for my ideas.

SECTION 3

Time

Time and tide wait for no man.

—Proverb

The ebb and flow of the ocean's tides is like the passing of time in architectural practice. The lapsing of time is the incoming tide that rushes to swallow the beach during a winter storm. The lagging of time is the summer wave that abandons the shore at low tide, leaving a desert's expanse of white-hot sand between land and water. Like the ocean, time is a two-faced player in architectural practice: At once, there is too much and not enough of it.

Yet, if we recall a pleasant day at the beach when we played at the water's edge, we will better understand how to regard time. At first, the waves knocked us down. Then, with practice and experience, we learned to ride their might to carry us ashore. Such is time in architectural practice. Athough we cannot control its passing, just as we cannot stop the cycle of waves that are here and gone, we can learn to go with its flow. Section 3: Time shows us how to keep pace with fleeting time.

3 TIME: WASTING IT

 3.1 Avoiding Repeated Mistakes

How can I avoid repeating the same mistakes?

A mistake is an opportunity to do something over, better than the first time. To ensure that your next try will be better than the last, Edwin C. Bliss, in *Getting Things Done*, recommends employing a military maneuver called an *after-action report* in which you record what happened during a significant occurrence that is likely to recur. After-action reports are appropriate for meetings, telephone conversations, interviews—with both clients and employees—and presentations and lectures. In a sense, they are similar to the pages that may collect in a journal or diary, in which you are candid about circumstances that arise in life. Do the following.

THREE LISTS FOR AVOIDING REPEATED MISTAKES

After an occurrence that is likely to recur, do the following:
1. List everything you did right.
2. List everything you did wrong.
3. List several ways to improve the results of the occurrence next time.

File the lists for future reference.

Handling Telephone Calls

Are there any tips for handling telephone calls more quickly and efficiently?

Communicating with people is fundamental to the success of your architectural practice. The telephone is an instrument of this communication. Using it effectively greatly benefits your practice. Using it inefficiently wastes time.

First, think about how you regard a telephone call by answering the following questions:

◆ How much of an interruption do you consider an incoming telephone call? Are you able to return from an incoming call to the task at hand without having to backtrack to find where you left off?

◆ Are you able to place an outgoing telephone call without backtracking on the task at hand?

Regardless of the way you view telephone calls—as welcome or unwelcome interruptions—you can deal with them more quickly and efficiently. After all, do you really want to break your concentration while calculating structural loads to field a call from a salesperson pitching photocopier toner?

See C.6 Telephone Log Form
See C.7 Telephone Conversation Record Form
See C.8 Telephone Message Form

FOUR WAYS TO MANAGE TELEPHONE CALLS

1. Log your calls.

Over the course of several days, log incoming and outgoing telephone calls. Review the log and ask yourself

- Am I being interrupted by unwanted incoming telephone calls from solicitors? How can I limit such interruptions?
- Do I need to be making all these outgoing calls? Could someone else make them, or could I contact people through alternate means such as letters or e-mail?

2. Screen your calls.

Screen your calls to ward off solicitors. Use your answering machine to screen calls. Let voice mail pick up your calls for an hour or two at a time. Use caller ID to keep track of welcome versus unwelcome calls; you may be surprised at the ratio.

3. Bank your calls.

Instead of making telephone calls as the mood strikes, thereby interrupting a block of thinking time, make all your calls in one sitting. Edwin C. Bliss, in *Getting Things Done*, recommends calling businesspeople just before lunch or at the end of the day when they are about to leave the office and are less likely to be long-winded.

4. Time your calls.

On beginning a telephone conversation, make a mental note of the time. Do the same on ending. Jot down the duration of the call. Or keep a timing device near the phone to determine the exact duration of the call.

Each month, long-distance call providers can list each call made and its duration according to accounting codes, based on your project numbers. If you are working on an hourly basis, you need to keep track of time spent on telephone calls for billing purposes. You may be surprised to see how much time you are spending on the telephone for a particular project.

In an effort to seem available to my clients when I first opened my practice, I answered telephone calls at all hours of the day and night. A barrage of calls from solicitors took away valuable time from my architecture projects, keeping me from meeting my obligations to my clients in the long run. I work hard to build a rapport with the people with whom I collaborate. While the telephone is a great device for doing this, I use it with a keen awareness of time.

Playing Telephone Tag

How can I cut down on playing telephone tag?

When you need to discuss an urgent matter, playing telephone tag can be frustrating. On the other hand, telephone tag can be used as a time-delaying tactic not to act on a bothersome matter. In our overbooked lives, it is a device of procrastination, which may or may not have a place in the balancing act of your architectural practice.

<table>
<tr><td>

MUSING

▼

So accustomed to answering machines and voice mail are we that we regard any first telephone call as the first domino to fall in the business game of telephone tag.

</td></tr>
</table>

If playing telephone tag annoys you, state explicitly your expectations in the messages you leave. If you know that you will be available to receive a return call at a certain time, say so. If you fear that the wrong person will hear an explicit message or that it may be lost, then playing telephone tag will be part of your future. Accept it.

Answering machines and voice mail allow you to make contact, albeit electronic, with the party you are calling; the telephone could be ringing off the hook. Your well-delivered messages are brief, to the point, and can get the desired results, unlike live conversations, which can ramble.

Answering machines and voice mail have advantages over receptionists or secretaries because your explicit messages will not be misstated by inaccurate note-takers.

Cutting Down Time at the Post Office

How can I spend less time on line at the post office?

There are several ways to spend less time at the post office, depending on the number and size of individual pieces of mail you generate. Try these.

FOUR WAYS TO SPEND LESS TIME IN LINE AT THE POST OFFICE

1. Purchase an inexpensive postal scale to determine postage requirements for outgoing mail. You can order stamps through USA Philatelic at 1.800.STAMP24 or through your local post office. Ask your postal carrier for an order form, or pick one up at your local post office.

2. Purchase a supply of stamps in various denominations so that you can put exact or near-exact postage on your outgoing mail.

3. Have on hand priority mail and express mail envelopes and labels; you can stuff one-rate envelopes with anything you can fit into them.

> **CAUTION**
>
>
>
> For security reasons, any package over 16 ounces must be weighed and posted at the post office.

4. With correspondence sealed and posted, drop mail in a neighborhood mailbox or a mailbox at the local post office, or if you have friendly relationships with your postal carriers, ask them to take it.

TIP

Consider opening up an account with a courier service such as UPS or Federal Express, who pick up packages right at your office.

Keeping a Master To-Do List

How do I keep track of all the things I want to do and have to do?

Picture the buffet tables on a cruise ship, laden with everything from nutritious raw vegetables to delicious desserts. Imagine the menu that lists all the foods offered at that meal. Not about to eat all of them, you probably will pick and choose among them. Similarly, a master to-do list is a menu from which you pick and choose what to accomplish each day. Here's how to prepare a master to-do list.

FOUR COURSES OF A MASTER TO-DO LIST

1. Jot down every practical thing you must do.
2. Jot down every enjoyable thing you want to do.
3. Identify the categories that become apparent as you review your entries.
4. Arrange your entries in these categories.

Here is a list of what some of those categories may be.

25 POTENTIAL CATEGORIES FOR A MASTER TO-DO LIST

Architecture projects
Automobiles
Cleaning

Competitions
Correspondence
Courses
Errands
Invoices
Legal matters
Marketing
Meetings
Money matters
Office chores
Personal chores
Personal development
Pet projects
Portfolio
Professional development
Promotion
Purchases
Reading
Research
Resume
Teaching
Telephone calls
Travel
Visiting
Writing

See 3.6 Updating a Master To-Do List
See 3.7 Making a Daily To-Do List
See C.9 Master To-Do List Form

3.6 Updating a Master To-Do List

Now that I have a master to-do list, how do I keep it current?

Make updating your master to-do list part of your daily routine.

KEEPING YOUR MASTER TO-DO LIST CURRENT

1. Keep your master to-do list in a computer file.
2. Jot down new entries on a hard copy as they occur to you throughout the day.
3. Cross out entries that have been accomplished or attended to or that no longer have a place on the list for one reason or another.
4. Update your computer file when you get a chance, and print out a hard copy of it.

I have heard it said that to make lists is to insult one's intelligence. I disagree. Not to make lists is to insult one's intelligence. I have more important things than lists to fill my mind. How about you?

See 3.5 Keeping a Master To-Do List
See 3.7 Making a Daily To-Do List

Making a Daily To-Do List

How can I plan activities so that I feel as though I have actually accomplished something by the end of each day?

Make a daily to-do list. Here are four steps to keeping it.

FOUR STEPS TO KEEPING A DAILY TO-DO LIST

1. Cull entries from your master to-do list to accomplish in a day.
2. Organize them into like categories.
3. As the day progresses, cross out each entry as you complete it.
4. Transfer entries that remain at the end of the day to tomorrow's to-do list.

See 3.5   Keeping a Master To-Do List
See 3.6   Updating a Master To-Do List
See C.10 Daily To-Do List Form

MY VIEW I keep my master to-do list in a computer file. I write my daily to-do list on a blank form of my design. This way, I can dash it off at the end of the day or first thing in the morning without sitting at the computer. The life span of the daily to-do list is so short that it is not worth the time to enter it into the computer; if I use it correctly, it is obsolete by the end of the day.

Evaluating Your Use of Time

How do I determine whether I am in control of my time?

In *The Organized Executive*, Stephanie Winston offers a "Time Quotient Self-Report" to help you evaluate your use of time. You are in control of your time if the statements below apply to you most of the time.

TEN SIGNS THAT YOU ARE IN CONTROL OF YOUR TIME

1. You know what your two or three primary tasks are for the day when you begin work each day.
2. You accomplish your primary tasks by the end of the day.
3. You meet your deadlines.
4. You monitor your staff to ensure that they meet their deadlines.
5. You tackle your most difficult tasks when your energy is the highest.

MUSING

One day you'll be twiddling
your thumbs for lack of work; the next
your fingers will be worn to the bone
because of too much of it.

---

6. You delegate tasks to staff members.

7. You keep unauthorized interruptions to a maximum of three a day.

8. You avoid procrastination by tackling difficult tasks.

9. You return telephone calls when you say you will.

10. You tackle day-to-day tasks that reflect and support your bigger goals.

See 1.2 Writing a Mission Statement
See 2.1 Evaluating Yourself as a Boss
See 3.5 Keeping a Master To-Do List
See 3.7 Making a Daily To-Do List
See 3.9 Planning Time

3 TIME: SCHEDULING IT

Planning Time

Although I eventually get tasks done in due time, I am always trying to beat the clock and usually losing to it. How can I plan my day so that I complete tasks in the allotted time?

Allotting time for any given task and completing it within that time take practice. Only experience tells you how long it takes to complete routine tasks. A time-use flowchart offers a representative, and visual, sampling of how you spend your time so that you can plan it better. Make one and use it.

MAKING A TIME-USE FLOWCHART

Start with an 11 × 17 inch or larger piece of paper, oak tag, marker board, etc., oriented with a short side to the left, landscape style. Make a grid to represent your work week, a giant-sized piece of graph paper.

1. List the days of your work week from top to bottom, evenly spaced along the left side of the paper.
2. List the hours of your work day from left to right, evenly spaced along the top of the paper.
3. Make boxes to represent the hour-long blocks of your work week.

USING A TIME-USE FLOWCHART

MUSING

The elephant has the longest gestation period of any creature on earth. Seemingly, it is shorter than the time it takes to do anything in architectural practice.

Within each block, jot down a brief description of each task you begin at a point that represents the portion of the hour, for example, halfway for any task you begin on the half hour.

When you complete a task, draw a horizontal line from its description to its completion time. Mark this time with an arrowhead at the line's end.

At the end of the week, compare the lengths of the arrows to see where you spent most of your time. When you have to complete the same or a similar task, you will have an idea of how much time to allow for it.

See 3.8 Evaluating Your Use of Time

Keeping Meetings on Time

Are there any tips for keeping meetings on time and on track?

You hold a meeting to seek results from the people who can deliver them. As an architect, you will participate in a variety of meetings on a regular basis:

◆ First-time meeting with clients
◆ Regular meetings with clients
◆ Staff meetings
◆ Meetings with consultants: accountants, bankers, lawyers, etc.
◆ Meetings with contractors and tradespeople
◆ Meetings with salespeople

There are formal meetings, held around a table, and informal meetings, held around a hole in the ground. Regardless of with whom and where you meet, prepare for meetings the same way. By preparing for meetings and adhering to time schedules, you will make them brief, lively, and productive. Here's how to keep meetings on track.

SEVEN STEPS FOR KEEPING MEETINGS ON TIME AND ON TRACK

1. Prepare brief agendas for meetings, outlining topics and setting time limits for them.
2. Circulate agendas ahead of time, or at least make participants aware of them, to allow attendees to prepare for their participation in meetings.

3. Begin meetings at the appointed times, despite the absence of latecomers, who will learn to arrive on time.
4. Ask staff members who arrive last to take the minutes of the meeting.
5. Watch the clock, adhering to time limits set on agendas.
6. Avoid digressions during discussions of topics.
7. Announce when allotted times for meetings are up, even if you must continue them a little longer.

See 3.11 Getting Results from Meetings

Getting Results from Meetings

Once a meeting is over, how do I ensure that the topics discussed will be addressed by the attendees?

To conclude a meeting, set a date then and there either for the next meeting or for when your colleagues will get back to you with their responses, reports, results, etc. This strategy encourages productivity.

See 3.10 Keeping Meetings on Time
See C.11 Meeting Notes Form

3 TIME: SCHEDULING IT

Scheduling Success

As a result of trying to build my business, I am a sole practitioner who has become a twenty-four-hour-a-day, seven-day-a-week architect. I answer the telephone from 7:30 in the morning until 10:30 at night. I meet with clients during the day, in the evenings, and on both Saturday and Sunday. I love my work, but it is consuming me. I am worried that if I don't continue to work all the time, I won't succeed. Any thoughts?

If you continue to work all the time, you will succeed in exhausting yourself. The 24/7 architect is bred in the architecture school design studio, where "all-nighters" provide the time needed to produce the amount of work required for projects. Much learning is compressed within a semester at school, but a semester quickly ends in a few months. Your practice ends at retirement.

You cannot sustain a lifelong career with unhealthy work habits. Therefore, pace yourself to handle all the roles you take on as a practitioner. To pace yourself, establish a schedule for yourself. Although not easy to do at first, it becomes easier to stick to with practice. Here are ten suggestions for establishing a schedule for yourself.

TEN TIPS FOR SCHEDULING SUCCESS

1. Opt to turn off the telephone for an hour or two to concentrate on work.

TIP

▼

Impose breaks on
your hectic schedule
by dividing your time
into manageable
daily, weekly,
monthly, and yearly
blocks of time in
which to complete
your work.

2. Choose not to meet with clients on Sunday or some other day of the week.

3. Decide not to work at all on Sunday, Saturday, or one afternoon during the work week.

4. Determine the evenings during the week that you will or will not schedule meetings.

5. Establish regular coffee breaks and lunch and dinner hours.

6. Set a time that you absolutely must stop work each day.

7. Take a walk or exercise at the same time every day.

8. Close your office on national holidays, religious holidays, or your birthday, even if you use these days to catch up on work.

9. Plan a vacation week or two or three, even if you do not have concrete plans.

10. Announce your schedule by mailing a schedule of office closings to your clients.

Once you've made a schedule, stick to it!

Bringing Order to Your Practice

3.13

How do I bring order to my practice without compromising my creativity?

Order in the architecture practice is not anathema to creativity. It makes room for it. The solutions to the problems presented in *The Architect's Business Problem Solver* are not intended to regiment you but rather to free you to design and build good architecture as you define it. Organizing your practice, both conceptually and physically, allows you the time to attend to your projects. Put first things first.

See 1.2   Writing a Mission Statement
See 1.3   Articulating Your Practice Values
See 1.4   Designing a Road Map
See 1.5   Outlining a Business Plan.
See 1.6   Strategizing for Success
See 1.7   Organizing Your Firm
See 1.8   Developing a Marketing Plan
See 3.5   Keeping a Master To-Do List
See 3.7   Making a Daily To-Do List
See 3.8   Evaluating Your Use of Time
See 3.9   Planning Time
See 3.14 Getting Organized

Getting Organized

How will I know when I am organized?

You are organized when you perceive the following.

A DOZEN SIGNS OF AN ORGANIZED INDIVIDUAL

1. You know what your two or three most important accomplishments will be for any given day because you keep master and daily to-do lists.
2. You concentrate on work at hand because you have developed a routine to avoid interruption.
3. You concentrate on the big picture—designing architectural projects, running the business, growing your practice—because you do not get bogged down with busywork.
4. You avoid crises of time because you avoid procrastinating on assignments.
5. You remember and keep appointments because you keep an appointment calendar and include appointments on your to-do lists.
6. You respond to correspondence and make return telephone calls promptly because you have devised a system to do so.
7. You retrieve any paper from your desk within 1 minute because your desk is not littered with nonessential materials.
8. You or your staff retrieves a file from the file cabinet or the computer within 5 minutes because you have an organized retrieval system.

9. You complete or are handed concise and clear-cut assignments on time because you outline their purposes, enumerate their goals, set their deadlines, and monitor their progress.
10. You work only on your assignments, not your staff's, because you hire capable individuals.
11. You complete work in your office because you do not want it to infiltrate your home life.
12. You deal with incoming mail, magazines, and newspapers because you do not want to accumulate clutter.

3.15 Lagging Time

As a sole practitioner, it takes me longer to produce my work than someone with a staff. How can I broach this topic so that clients do not regard it as a liability?

First, stop regarding sole practitionership as a liability. Your undivided attention on clients' projects assures them that the standards of quality and care are the highest. That it takes a little longer for you to produce their works is characteristic of a practice in which you bear sole responsibility for everything. Promote this as an asset.

The tips, tactics, and techniques throughout this book are aimed at helping you speed through the more mundane aspects of running your practice. Use them, and you may find that you have more time and a clearer conscience to concentrate on your architecture projects.

Money

Bankroll

Loans

Fees

Salaries

Expenses

Taxes

Money: Will it be the ship that comes in or the ship that passes in the night?

On deciding to offer architectural services for compensation, we decide to come to terms with money in all its respects. On receiving that first installment from a paying client, a far-off light on the dark horizon signals to each of us that we may just be able to make our respective livings as architect practitioners. But will the beacon fade into the distance on a passing ship, or will its light grow brighter as it heads toward each of our ports? Clearly, it is up to us to determine where the gold light shines.

In the waters of architectural practice, financial obstacles abound. To pay little heed to these money matters is to ignore potential threats to our practices. Such icebergs can tear holes in the hulls of our practices, causing them to take on water and, ultimately, to sink before reaching their destinations.

Yet steering our practices through a sea of financial concerns need not mean treacherous travel. Rather, if we chart our courses carefully, with alternate routes and safety measures detailed in advance, our journeys will lead us to prosperity. Section 4: Money points us in the right direction.

4 BANKROLL

4.1 Launching a Practice

What are the costs associated with launching a practice?

In *How to Start and Operate Your Own Design Firm*, Albert W. Rubeling, Jr., offers a list that is helpful in determining the costs associated with launching a practice. It is adapted below. Before launching your firm, try to determine whether the following items apply and how much each will cost.

- **Business license**
- **Professional license**
- **Rental deposit on office**
- **Telephone installation and deposits**
- **Utility deposits**
- **Insurance**
  Health
  General liability
  Professional liability
  Life
  Theft
  Disability
- **Legal**
  Initial consultation
  Form of business papers
- **Accounting**
  Initial consultation
  Format resolution

♦ **Dues for professional organizations**
Local
State
National
♦ **Advertising**
Advertisements
Brochures
♦ **Stationery**
Business cards
Letterhead
Envelopes
Mailing labels
♦ **Equipment**
Computer
Computer software
Printer(s)
Scanner
Typewriter
Telephone(s)
Answering machine
Facsimile machine
Calculator
Photocopier
Blueprint machine
Camera
Stereo
Television
Videocassette recorder
♦ **Supplies**
Pencils, pens
Toner
Ink cartridges, ribbons
Paper(s)
Drafting implements
Paper clips

Rubber bands

Stapler and staples

Notebooks

♦ **Furniture**

Desk(s)

Drafting table(s)

Computer station

Chair(s)

Lamp(s)

Bookcases

File cabinets

Storage cabinets

See 4.2   Getting Your Nest Egg Together

See 4.3   Determining Financial Needs

See 4.4   Finding Startup Money

See C.12 Startup Money Checklist Form

BANKROLL

Getting Your Nest Egg Together

Before I launch my practice, how much money should I save up?

As a rule of thumb, have a year's worth of overhead in hand before launching your practice. Michael Gill and Sheila Paterson, authors of *Fired Up! From Corporate Kiss-Off to Entrepreneurial Kick-Off,* strongly suggest saving two years' worth of overhead before you hang your shingle.

Besides the practical matter of having funds to operate, there is a psychological advantage to having money saved up: You will not be as desperate to take on any and every project just to keep yourself going.

See 4.1   Launching a Practice
See 4.3   Determining Financial Needs
See 4.4   Finding Startup Money

TIP

Approach your banker for a business
loan when you are still employed,
since as a self-employed individual,
you are considered a greater risk.

4 BANKROLL

4.3 Determining Financial Needs

If I open an architectural practice, I must support it as well as my family and me. How do I determine the financial needs required to support my personal life?

Come up with figures for the following personal expenses to determine your monthly operating costs:

◆ **Residence**
Monthly payment
Taxes
Insurance

◆ **Utilities**
Water
Telephone
Heat and air conditioning
Electricity

◆ **Clothing**
Yours
Spouse's
Children's

◆ **Food**

◆ **Automobile**
Payment
Gas
Maintenance

Insurance
Registration

◆ **Credit**
Credit cards
Installment loans
Student loans

◆ **Other**
Life insurance
Education
Medical and dental
Taxes
Recreation
Travel
Donations
Health insurance

See C.13 Financial Needs Checklist Form

 # Finding Startup Money

Where can I get startup money to launch and run my practice?

Most, if not all, of your startup money comes from your own reserve because banks are reluctant to lend money to a business without a track record. Thus you will most likely have to work at your current job to save up money to launch your practice. Investing your own money in a new practice sends a signal to observers that you truly believe in what you are doing and are willing to take a personal financial risk to do it.

Some other possible sources of startup money are

♦ Equity loans on real estate that you own
♦ Life insurance policies that you cash in
♦ Personal loans from family and friends

LOANS

Borrowing Money

What are the basic principles for borrowing money to expand my practice?

Here are 10 tips for borrowing money adapted from *The Macmillan Small Business Handbook* by Mark Stevens.

TEN TIPS FOR BORROWING MONEY

1. Apply for loans at several banks, maintaining relationships with these sources over the years to improve the odds of keeping the flow of money open at all times.
2. Solicit loans from banks that are accustomed to dealing with architectural firms.
3. Shop for a loan before you actually need it.
4. Apply for the full amount of the loan up front instead of several smaller loans that require a bank to dole out money in installments. This approach ensures that you will not be without money at a critical point in your practice.
5. Borrow more money than you think you need to account for exceeding your projections. Try 25 percent.
6. Treat borrowing money as part of the managerial process of your practice. Build reserves of money to have at your disposal.
7. Follow up on the bank's decision on your loan. Ask the banker when approval is expected, and follow up on that date.

8. Time lending requests to coordinate with favorable events in your business, such as landing the commission for a big project.
9. Look for alternative means of getting money in lean economic times.
10. Look beyond the interest rates of the loans you are comparing to the amount of available financing and the terms of the loan. Favor the lender offering the best mix of financing features.

See 4.6 Getting a Business Loan

4 LOANS

Getting a Business Loan

Are there tips to ensure that I will get a business loan for my practice?

Take steps to impress bankers. Winning their confidence helps you stand out from the crowd. Begin building a relationship with your banker by inviting him or her to your business to observe firsthand what makes your practice tick. Then follow the five steps below to solidify your budding relationship.

FIVE STEPS IN BUILDING A RELATIONSHIP WITH A BANKER

1. Inform your banker of business difficulties when they arise. Do not try to cover them up.
2. Give your banker reasons to share your enthusiasm about your practice by sending along positive press for him or her to place in your credit file.
3. Pay off loans in advance. This leads to goodwill.
4. Demonstrate your ability to personally guarantee business loans. Prepare financial statements that list personal assets including stocks, bonds, and cash. Bankers want evidence of net worth beyond a borrower's house and business.
5. Volunteer comprehensive information about your business such as financial statements for the past 3 years and 3-year cash flow projections.

4 FEES

Broaching the Topic of Fees with Clients

How can I broach the topic of fees with prospective clients before waiting to address it in my proposal?

To broach the topic of fees with prospective clients before waiting to address it in your proposal, compose a letter of introduction that you give to them at your initial meeting. Here are the parts that may comprise such a letter.

FOUR PARTS OF A LETTER ABOUT FEES

1. An overview of the typical phases of a project as you define them or as defined by the American Institute of Architects
2. A forecast of the amount of fees to anticipate
3. A formula for establishing the target construction budget
4. A discussion of the gathering of background information pertinent to the project, such as recording the existing conditions of a project site

With this letter, enclose the following.

TWO ENCLOSURES IN A LETTER ABOUT FEES

1. A summary of phases for a typical project that briefly explains the goals of each phase

2. A list of typical phases for a project with applicable fees: a fee schedule

See 2.15 Writing a Proposal
See 2.18 Negotiating an Agreement

MUSING

**Even though I am good at what I do,
I am poor at what I do.**

FEES

Offering Design Counseling Services

After working in the city for a number of years, I opened my own architectural practice in my hometown with the hope of getting some big projects there. How can I bring in some money to sustain my practice before landing those big commissions?

To start taking in money or to supplement fees from your commissioned projects, consider offering design counseling services. *Design counseling*, simply a fancy name for consulting on an hourly basis, is an interesting and effective way to tap into the architecture market. It is different from regular architectural services because you are not commissioned to design an entire project; rather, you are hired to offer advice about some aspect of architecture in 1-hour increments. By making yourself available on an hourly basis, you give prospective clients of architectural services the chance to sample working with you before making a commitment to a project.

In all kinds of architectural projects, the need exists for experts to help clients establish goals for their projects. As a design counselor, you can enter the picture early by helping clients to determine the programs for their projects. If these projects go forward, you are a likely candidate for the commissions.

In the residential market, where homeowners are sometimes reluctant to hire architects, design counseling allows you to prove your worth by acting as a sounding board for homeowners who need an artistic eye or some technical advice. Clients pleased with their design counseling experience may see the advantages of hiring you to design their projects.

The greatest benefit of design counseling is that it compensates you immediately for advice you may have given for free previously during initial consultations with clients to discuss their projects. With a little practice, you can turn many inquiries about your service into design counseling sessions. The pin money such sessions provide can be the difference between making ends meet or not.

Guidelines, at 800-634-7779, offers a home-study course in design counseling.

See 2.10 Embellishing Your Yellow Pages Listing
See Appendix A

Getting Clients to Pay

I have sent a couple of months' worth of statements to clients who have yet to pay them. Although I am continuing to work on their project, I am beginning to worry about not getting paid. What can I do?

Slow-paying clients are one of the greatest frustrations of architectural practice. Even more frustrating is having to combine your role as designer with that of bill collector, one of the more disdainful aspects of architecture as business.

Although it is easy to jump to the conclusion that a client's slow payment indicates dissatisfaction with your service, several reasons exist for why payments seem to arrive so slowly. They relate to the types of clients you have.

If your clients are corporations, health care facilities, religious organizations, etc., approval from someone in authority may be required before you get paid. Often, it is simply the shuffling of paperwork that holds up your payment, especially if your invoice must go from one department to another and if payments are made on only certain days of the month.

If your clients are homeowners, their hectic schedules may cause them to put off paying you. Monthly bills such as telephone, utilities, and mortgages may take precedence over your bill, which, besides being one of their bigger expenditures for the month, may be regarded as an extra to pay when they can. They may have to wait to get paid themselves before paying you.

Such explanations, although legitimate, seem to excuse your clients for not meeting the terms of their agreement. What about the bills you have to pay?

In rare instances, failure by clients to pay you does indeed indicate dissatisfaction with your service. Confront this situation head on.

Here is list of ways to get clients to pay you on time.

EIGHT WAYS TO GET CLIENTS TO PAY ON TIME

TIP

In situations where residential clients seem unable to pay your monthly fees in full, set up an installment plan that coincides with the days of the month they receive their paychecks.

1. Establish due dates for payments in your agreements with clients. The universally accepted practice is 30 days from the date of your invoice.
2. Follow up your first statements to clients to make sure they understand your billing procedure. Or assign an employee this task as a regular assignment. If you do not have employees, consider asking a friend to do this in order to distance yourself from this basic aspect of practice.
3. Assign an employee or ask a friend to follow up regularly on all statements of services rendered that you send out.
4. Ask for initial payments that cover expenses for about a month's work on any project. In this way, if a client refuses to pay, credit the initial payment toward the work you have completed.
5. Design your monthly statements to stand out from the other paperwork you send to clients, especially if you believe that your statements are getting lost among the many papers you send.
6. Time monthly statements with meetings, memoranda, or best of all, the delivery of drawings for projects. Even though you are providing a service based on your expertise, clients like to feel that they are paying for something tangible.

7. If clients fail to pay in a timely manner, devise a cordial reminder note to put them on notice. Place a telephone call, or have an employee or friend call to inquire if there is a problem with your service.

8. If clients fail to pay, suspend service on their project and focus on another until you are paid. If too much time goes by without getting paid, inform your clients in writing that you have suspended service.

See 2.23   Defining the Effective Architect and Client Relationship
See 5.13   Stocking Stationery
See C.14   Billable Hours Tally Sheet Form
See C.17   Fees and Reimbursables Tally Sheet Form

4 SALARIES

Affording a New Employee

Although I have decided to increase my staff by hiring a new employee, I wonder whether I can afford one. How can I justify this added expense?

There are two methods for justifying a new employee: qualitative and quantitative. The qualitative method is discussed in Section 2: People. The quantitative method is discussed below.

QUANTITATIVE METHOD TO JUSTIFY A NEW EMPLOYEE

Putting a dollar and cents amount on a new employee is the quantitative method to justify a new employee. Stephanie Winston, in *The Organized Executive*, uses a cost and benefit formula that helps determine the amount of money you could pay a new employee based on the amount of money it costs for you to handle certain tasks. It is adapted here.

1. Collect 2 to 3 weeks of daily to-do lists.
2. Check off all tasks that may be delegated to a new employee.
3. Divide the tasks into two categories: managerial and clerical.
4. Group similar tasks within categories into blocks.
5. Tally time spent on the tasks in each block.

Before proceeding, ask yourself whether the tasks in any of the blocks could be assigned to existing staff. Go on to the next steps to determine a salary for your new employee.

6. Figure out how much the tasks cost by multiplying the hours you spent doing them by your hourly salary.
7. Come up with a weekly average by dividing the preceding amount by the number of weeks it took to accomplish the tasks.
8. Multiply the weekly average by 52 to come up with the yearly salary that would pay someone to complete these tasks.

See 2.31 Justifying a New Employee

 **Giving Raises**

How do I determine whether or not to give an employee a raise?

Use the employee review meeting as the basis for giving a raise. Base your decision on the following.

FOUR CONSIDERATIONS IN GIVING RAISES

After your employee review meeting, give thought to the following four considerations:

1. The employee's current level of performance
2. The amount of improvement or decline demonstrated by the employee since the last review
3. The way the employee has performed in comparison with other employees in the same position
4. The going rate for employees in similar positions in similar firms

See 2.38 Reviewing Employee Job Performance

Establishing Open Accounts

Although I don't have cash or my checkbook to pay my blueprinter on the spot, I don't want to rack up expenses on my credit card. How do I get businesses to bill me for products purchased or services rendered?

Establish open accounts with the businesses you deal with on a regular basis. Typically, you have up to 30 days to pay your bills, which helps contribute to a steadier cash flow.

To open such accounts, you usually need several business references, which can be difficult to come by if you are just starting out. Try approaching a local business with which you have a personal relationship, such as the blueprinter who printed work for your portfolio.

Keep your local accounts current, and you will be able to use them as references for mail-order businesses.

TIP

▼

If businesses give you trouble establishing open accounts, suggest putting a credit card number on record as a sort of collateral. In this way, they have the option to bill past-due amounts to your credit card.

 # Opting for a Business Telephone Line

4.13

If I work out of my house, what is the advantage of a business telephone line over a residential line?

A business telephone line entitles you to a free listing in the Yellow Pages of your local telephone book. Such a listing helps you establish a presence in your local geographic area. Usually, a business line costs more than a private line, however.

Unlimited local calls are a standard feature of private-line service, whereas local calls on a business line are charged to your account in message units, any portion of a predetermined increment. For example, if you make a 2-minute local call on a business line, you may be charged for a full 5 minutes.

See 2.10 Embellishing Your Yellow Pages Listing
See 4.15 Listing in the Yellow Pages
See 4.16 Paying for Voice Mail

 # Signing up for Telephone Accounting Codes

When I tally reimbursables for my projects each month, it takes me a long time to determine which long-distance telephone calls belong to what clients. Is there a shortcut?

When signing up for long-distance telephone service, pick a provider that arranges your monthly telephone bill according to accounting codes.

Each month, your bill will group and tally long-distance telephone calls by accounting codes that you make up, usually the project numbers. Every time you dial a long distance number, a tone prompts you to enter the accounting code to identify the reason for your call or to assign it to a particular project.

Ask your long-distance provider how many digits you can use to make up accounting codes, which you also can use to track calls for general office functions such as advertising, marketing, and promotion. Also, try to find a provider that tracks toll calls within your state.

Listing in the Yellow Pages

How do I get listed in the Yellow Pages of my local telephone book?

To get a free listing in the Yellow Pages, subscribe to business service through your local telephone company. Business service entitles you to a one-line, plain-faced entry under the Yellow Pages heading of your choice. For an additional charge to your monthly telephone bill, you can zip up your entry with a bold listing or extra lines to characterize your business. Ask your sales representative for promotions that the telephone company is running at the moment.

See 2.10 Embellishing Your Yellow Pages Listing
See 4.13 Opting for a Business Telephone Line

Paying for Voice Mail

Working out of my home, I have both private and business telephone lines. Aware that I am charged message units on my business line by my telephone company, I tried to save money by making local calls on my private line, which has unlimited service. Unfortunately, my monthly phone bill has not gone down significantly. What's up?

Do you have voice mail? Voice mail messages are charged to your account in message units. Therefore, every time a caller leaves a message, you pay for it. Continue to use your private line for local calls and to check messages on your business line. Or consider purchasing an answering machine if you do not want voice mail messages charged to your account in message units.

See 4.13 Opting for a Business Telephone Line

4.17 # Paying Monthly Bills

Monthly bill paying is a time-consuming affair that seems to take me away from my architecture for a day or more. And I never seem to have enough money to pay all my bills at one time. Any tips?

Instead of taking a day or more at the end of the month to pay bills, balance your checkbook, and account for expenses, try spreading these activities out over the course of a month as outlined below.

PAYING BILLS OVER THE COURSE OF A MONTH

1. List the due dates of your monthly bills: telephone, electric, etc.
2. List the due dates of your quarterly bills: taxes, etc.
3. List the due dates of your half-yearly bills: health insurance, etc.
4. List the due dates of your yearly bills: automobile registration, etc.

See where the due dates fall, and identify a pattern that allows you to pay bills three times a month. For instance, consider paying bills on or about the eighth, eighteenth, and twenty-eighth of every month. Account for expenses and balance your checkbook on one of these days, depending on when your canceled checks are returned to you.

Only a steady stream of money coming in alleviates cash worries, but paying bills three times a month may jibe better with the pace of incoming money. This is why it is called *cash flow!*

See 4.20 Tracking Expenses

MUSING

**Lack of money is the greatest cause
of procrastination.**

Picking Checks

Should I opt for a business check book with oversized checks? Is there a practical way to keep track of checks without using one of those tiny check registers the banks give out with their checks?

Personal-sized checks are convenient to carry when you run errands. Consider making your own business-style checkbook using a three-ring binder and a five-column analysis pad in which to record transactions.

Label columns of the analysis pad with the categories: date, explanation, check number, debit, credit, fees/interest, and balance. Use it as you would a regular check register. It is harder to misplace and easier to use than a small checkbook. Its larger format gives you a better overview of your expenses and is easy to shelve.

If you use this system but still carry checks with you from time to time, remember to record your transaction on the cardboard backing. Transfer it to your big book later.

See 4.19 Buying Checks through Mail Order

Buying Checks through Mail-Order

Should I purchase my checks through one of those mail-order companies instead of through my bank?

Checks from mail-order companies are cheaper. Look for advertisements in the backs of magazines.

The first time you order, you will be required to send a blank check from your bank along with your payment. If you are worried about sending a blank check as well as a signed check, pay with a postal money order, on which your signature is not required.

Use the deposit slips these companies provide even though they are not in duplicate; your bank will provide a receipt.

See 4.18 Picking Checks

 **Tracking Expenses**

How do I keep track of expenses throughout the year in order to make tallying expenses easier at tax time?

Although there are computer programs to help you track expenses, you can set up a hands-on system yourself.

SEVEN STEPS TO TRACKING EXPENSES

1. Identify categories that require listing on Schedule C of Form 1040 Individual Tax Return, for example, S for stationery and office supplies and T for telephone service, long-distance telephone calls, cellular telephone calls, etc.
2. Fill a three-ring binder with hole-punched pockets, one for every imaginable category of expense as well as one for fees and reimbursables.
3. Put a piece of paper in each pocket, labeled with the abbreviation for the category.
4. Place monthly bills in a pocket at the front of the binder, noting their amounts and due dates on a sheet of paper labeled with the month.
5. When fees and reimbursables come in, log them in on the appropriate sheet of paper.
6. When you balance your checkbook at the end of every month, write in the date, amount paid, and method of payment for each expenditure on its appropriate sheet in the three-ring binder. Remember to account for charges made on credit cards.

7. Write an abbreviation next to each entry in your checkbook to show that you have accounted for it in your tracking system.

At the end of each month, your sheets will show your expenses and income. At the end of the year, tally up the entries on all your lists to determine your yearly expenses in a particular category. Show these expenses on the appropriate line of Schedule C, Form 1040.

See 4.17 Paying Monthly Bills
See 4.23 Reporting and Paying Taxes
See C.15 Individual Expense Record Form
See C.16 Automobile Mileage Record Form

4 EXPENSES

Saving Money on Buying Stuff

I seem to spend a small fortune every time I buy stationery and drafting supplies. These expenditures seem out of proportion to the fees I take in. How can I save money on buying this stuff?

You can spend a small fortune outfitting yourself with stationery, lined pads, pencils, and pens, not to mention drafting supplies. Mail-order catalogs offer great savings on such supplies. See Appendix B.

TIP

Stock up on stationery and drafting
supplies when exclusive catalogs
run sales.

Reviewing the Types of Taxes

What are the types of taxes?

Depending on the form of your business, report your income tax in one of a few ways.

See 4.23 Reporting and Paying Taxes

Besides income taxes, familiarize yourself with these other taxes:

▼ Self-Employment Tax

Self-employed individuals make payments to Social Security with self-employment tax, based on a percentage of your net profit from running a business. It is distinct from income tax. Sole proprietors and partners are liable for self-employment tax. Corporate stockholders are not. Self-employment tax is filed using Schedule SE of Form 1040.

▼ Estimated Income Tax

Sole proprietors and partners are liable for estimated tax. It is equivalent to the tax that was withheld from your paycheck when you were an employee at a firm.

Quarterly estimated tax payments are due on April 15, June 15, September 15, and January 15. Skip the January 15 payment if you file your yearly tax return with any balance due by January 31.

To estimate taxes, either figure your taxable income each quarter or base your taxes on last year's tax income, paying one quarter of that amount each quarter.

Form 1040 ES tells you how to file estimated taxes.

▼ Payroll taxes

If you have employees, concern yourself with three types of payroll taxes that are based on your employees' wages:

- Federal and state income taxes
- Social Security taxes (FICA)
- Federal and state unemployment taxes (FUTA)

▼ Income taxes

Income taxes are withheld on wages paid to an employee above a prescribed minimum, depending on the withholding allowances claimed by that employee on his or her W-2 Form. These taxes are collected quarterly, monthly, or biweekly, depending on the amount. Payments are made to the IRS on Form 501 through your bank.

The method for filing state withholdings is similar to other federal methods.

▼ Social Security taxes (FICA)

Payments made to Social Security on your employee's behalf are figured on a portion of wages paid to that employee. As the employer, you match the amount withheld from the employee's wages.

▼ Federal unemployment tax (FUTA)

You are required to pay federal unemployment tax on a certain amount of each employee's wages.

You are required to pay state unemployment taxes, too.

See 4.23 Reporting and Paying Taxes
See 4.24 Scheduling Tax Payments

4.23 Reporting and Paying Taxes

How and where do I report my business operations and pay taxes?

Report your business operations and pay taxes depending on the form of your business.

▼ Sole proprietor

If you are a sole proprietor, meaning that you are the sole owner of your business and that the business is not incorporated, report your business operations on Schedule C of Form 1040 Individual Tax Return.

▼ Partnership

If your practice is a partnership, the partnership itself is not liable for federal income tax; however, file Form 1065. You and your partner(s) report your share of profits on your individual Form 1040s.

▼ Corporation

If your practice is a corporation, file Form 1120 and pay taxes on the taxable income reported. Report your salary dividends from the corporation on your individual Form 1040.

If you run your business on the calendar year ending on December 31, your tax return is due April 15, just as it was when you were an employee. However, if you run your practice on a fiscal year, a 12-month period ending the last day of any month but December, your tax return is due on the fifteenth day of the fourth month following the end of that fiscal year.

See 4.22   Reviewing the Types of Taxes
See 4.24   Scheduling Tax Payments

Scheduling Tax Payments

When are tax payments due?

Taxes are due according to the schedule below for a calendar year. Withholdings taxes for employees are not indicated because due dates vary.

▼ January

15: Sole proprietor estimated tax due.
    Partnership estimated tax due.
    S corporation shareholder estimated tax due.

31: FICA and FUTA taxes due.
    W-2 Forms to employees.
    1099 Forms to consultants.

▼ March

15: Corporation income tax due.
    S corporation income tax due.

▼ April

15: Sole proprietor income tax due.
    Self-employment estimated tax due.
    Sole proprietor estimated tax due.
    Partnership estimated tax due.
    S corporation estimated tax due.
    Annual return of partnership income tax due.

30: FICA and FUTA taxes due.

▼ June

15: Sole proprietor estimated tax due.
   Partnership estimated tax due.
   S corporation estimated tax due.

▼ July

31: FICA and FUTA taxes due.

▼ September

15: Sole proprietor estimated tax due.
   Partnership estimated tax due.
   S corporation estimated tax due.

▼ October

31: FICA and FUTA taxes due.

See 4.22   Reviewing the Types of Taxes
See 4.23   Reporting and Paying Taxes

Choosing an Accounting Method

As I deposit payments for fees and reimbursables from my clients into my checking account and send payments out to vendors, how do I account for the money coming in and going out as it relates to my tax return? I've heard of accounting methods: cash or accrual. Which is right for me?

As a professional who offers a service, the cash method of accounting is probably right for you. Use this method to report all income received minus all expenses paid in cash. Income must be reported if it is constructively received, even though it is not in your actual possession as in the case of interest on a savings account. A charge on a credit card is an expense at the time it is incurred, even though you may pay it off over time.

4 TAXES

4.26 Learning about Taxes

I don't have an accountant yet because I just launched my practice and am testing the waters before laying out money for consultants. How can I learn what I need to know about taxes?

The IRS publishes many informational pamphlets to ensure that taxpayers meet their obligations. Contact the IRS at 800-829-3676. Also, those big, thick tax guides that you may have used to prepare your Form 1040 as an employee are helpful to business owners as well. Buy one.

See Appendix A.

MY VIEW Besides informational pamphlets from the IRS and tax guides from your local bookstore, computer tax preparation programs can be instructive. Although the several programs I used proved futile in preparing my tax returns themselves, they offered helpful and useful tidbits of information on preparing my own forms.

 # Establishing a Home Office

In launching my practice, I decided to set up shop in my house. Are there any considerations relative to the IRS that I should look into immediately?

Be aware of a few considerations relative to the IRS when you set up a practice in your house. Use the bywords *divide* and *separate*.

▼ Devote an entire room to your business

The IRS does not recognize a corner of a room as appropriate for a business-use-of-home deduction.

▼ Set up separate business and personal bank accounts

Pay all business expenses from your business account.

▼ Install a business telephone line

You can deduct all the expenses related to this phone.

TAXES

Handling a Tax Audit

How do I handle a tax audit?

Mark Stevens, in *The Macmillan Small Business Handbook*, offers the following six strategies for handling a tax audit.

SIX STRATEGIES FOR HANDLING A TAX AUDIT

1. Keep to the subject.
Answer only the questions from the tax examiner, staying within the narrow framework of his or her inquiry and not volunteering information.

2. Hire an accountant or a lawyer.
By removing yourself from the audit process and allowing an experienced consultant to handle it, you prevent your inexperience from negatively affecting the audit findings.

3. Bring documentation.
Paperwork that shows how deductions were calculated helps the tax examiner reconcile deductions on returns and saves time.

4. Direct attention toward documentation.
By focusing the examiner's attention on matters for which you have thorough and convincing documentation, you set the tone for a low-key audit with evidence of your honesty and accuracy.

5. Cooperate with the tax examiner.

Refrain from showing anger toward the tax examiner and resist trying to intimidate him or her as a strategy of arguing a case in your favor.

6. Appeal unfair findings.

Take your case to the IRS Appellate Division or courts, where appeals officers are authorized to settle cases likely to go against the IRS in court.

See 2.44 Hiring Consultants
See 2.45 Hiring an Accountant
See 2.47 Hiring a Lawyer

Stuff

**Scraps of dreams and duds of daring,
home-brought stuff from far sea-faring.**

—*Spring Song*
Bliss Carman

If the practice of architecture is a journey, then we must make room to stow the provisions we need and the treasures we discover along the way. Often our offices resemble shipwrecks, strewn with the flotsam and jetsam of practice: the latest gadgetry, the odd architectural artifact, and the reams and reams of paper that float across every horizontal surface from port to starboard side.

Paper can be both a boon to and the bane of our existence as practicing architects. Made into drawings, paper can become the sails of our destiny. In bulk, as in the seemingly innocent bundle of mail that arrives every day, paper can become the anchor that weighs us down.

Not really motivated by the argument that it is better to be tidy than untidy—we all possess different tolerance levels for messiness—Section 5: Stuff aims to buoy us up in an endless sea of paraphernalia by helping us to sort, sift, shift, and store the stuff we need, the stuff we make, and the stuff we get each and every day. In directing us through the stuff of architecture practice, it swiftly returns us to a more familiar place in front of our drafting boards.

STUFF: STORING

Keeping Your Office Shipshape

My office is in continual disarray. I literally abandon my desk every evening to return to an overwhelming mess in the morning. Although I complete my work, it is not without a lot of frustration: I always have to sort through a lot of stuff to get everything accomplished. How can I keep my office shipshape?

Working in an orderly environment supposedly provides positive psychological benefits. The practical reason for keeping your office organized is that it allows you to be more productive. While a mess may be distracting visually, having to sift through that mess simply wastes time. Moving stuff from here to there because you did not put it away and spending time sorting through piles of papers to find an important document take time away from your architecture projects. On a ship that rocks and rolls, provisions are battened down and stowed away so that they do not fall all over the place. Do the same in your architecture office.

DEFENDING AGAINST DISARRAY

There is a two-pronged approach to defend against disarray in your office.

▼ First Prong

Have a place for everything:

◆ Trays, boxes, or baskets for incoming and outgoing mail

- Bags, satchels, or cases for portfolios, cameras, projectors
- Bins, baskets, or bags at every location where trash and recyclables are generated
- Filing cabinets for folders, drawings, and project literature
- Storage cabinets for office and drafting supplies and product samples
- Open shelving for large items
- Bookcases for books, reference materials, building codes, periodicals, and ring binders
- Racks for drawing tubes, rolls of paper, model-making materials, and coats

▼ Second Prong

Work to keep everything in its place:
- Handle incoming mail immediately.
- Put loose papers in their place.
- Empty trash and recycling receptacles before they overflow.
- Use ring binders or another adaptable organizing system for keeping like items together.
- Keep out only those things which you are working on at the moment.

See Appendix B

TIP

Five minutes, fifteen minutes, or a half an hour before you leave your office for the day, take the time to clear your desk of writing and drafting implements, project files, mail, and other loose papers.

I worked in an architectural firm where everything but the drawing taped to my drafting table had to be put away before I left for the day. I believe this custom came about as a result of a fire in the office, which spread rapidly and consumed everything in sight. To this day, I stow everything, if just to protect it.

TIP

**To give the illusion of order
in an office littered with the stuff
of ongoing projects, decorate the walls
with neatly arranged diplomas,
licenses, photographs, and drawings
in frames, as well as interesting
architectural artifacts and collectibles.**

STUFF: BUYING

Finding Good Stuff

Where do I get good stuff?

To get good stuff through mail order, see Appendix B.

Setting up a Filing System

Here I am, on my own for the first time, faced with organizing all the papers I'll need to be a success. How do I set up a filing system from scratch?

To set up a filing system from scratch, use a model. Think about the filing systems at your previous places of work. What was good about them? What was bad about them? Do you want to use them as your models of efficiency? Or do you want to use them as examples to avoid?

If you need a little help setting up a filing system, try the seven-step system below.

SEVEN STEPS TO SET UP A FILING SYSTEM

1. Assemble your materials.
Purchase hanging folders, hanging folder labels, third-cut file folders, file-folder labels (if desired), label-making software for your computer, or a broad-tipped marker.

2. Determine categories.
Make up broad categories for the hanging folders that represent your practice, such as project files and vendors. Make up more specific categories for the file folders, such as correspondence or the names of individual vendors whose receipts must be filed.

3. Make labels.

Make labels using a computer font with large, simple letters or hand lettering with easy-to-read block letters.

4. Arrange hanging folders.

Arrange hanging folders according to like categories. Group project files together, arranged either numerically by project number or alphabetically by project name. Place all office-related hanging folders together: taxes, vendors, insurance, résumés, etc.

5. Organize file folders.

Place all papers in file folders, arranging them chronologically from most to least recent.

6. Arrange file folders.

Arrange file folders alphabetically within their designated hanging folders.

7. Make an index.

Once all the files are arranged, make an index that lists your hanging-folder categories and the file folder categories within them. State where these files are kept. Consider diagraming your filing system as a visual key to it. This may be as simple as a sketch of a single filing cabinet or a map of multiple filing cabinets in and around your office.

See 5.4 Categorizing Your Files
See 5.5 Keeping a Filing System
See 5.11 Sorting Piles of Papers
See Appendix B

5 PAPER: FILES

5.4 Categorizing Your Files

Papers are beginning to accumulate in my office: correspondence to clients, transmittals to general contractors, invoices from vendors, tax forms from the IRS, product literature from manufacturers. How do I go about organizing this barrage of papers?

As papers infiltrate your office, you will begin to identify categories into which you can organize your files. In deciding on general categories for your filing system, keep them broad. To do this, name them with single-word titles. These categories will organize your hanging folders. Within categories, try not to devise too many subcategories. Here are some possible file categories with the types of papers to file under them.

POSSIBLE FILE CATEGORIES

▼ Projects

Keep all papers relevant to your projects: from agreements to statements of services rendered.

▼ Taxes

Yearly tax returns
Sales and use tax forms
Estimated tax forms
Employee payroll taxes, W-2 Forms
Federal and state withholding records and forms

▼ Insurance

Life
Health
Car

▼ Vendors

Paid invoices for:
Stationery
Drafting supplies
Telephone service
Books
Credit cards

▼ People

Résumés from prospective employees
Résumés from consultants

▼ Advertising

Invoices from newspapers, magazines, flyers, public relations articles

▼ Products

▼ Organizations

AIA
NCARB

▼ Important papers

Office lease

▼ Stationery

Forms originals
Letterhead design
Postcard design
Brochure design

See 5.3 Setting up a Filing System
See 5.11 Sorting Piles of Paper

Keeping a Filing System

Do you have any tips for keeping a filing system?

There are several ways to keep a filing system at its best. Try them.

EIGHT WAYS TO KEEP A FILING SYSTEM AT ITS BEST

1. Avoid a miscellaneous category of files; it is a catch-all.
2. Consider color-coding your filing system. Hanging folders, file folders, labels, and of course, ink come in a variety of colors. Pick a different color for each category in your system. This will speed filing. At the very least, it is more visually appealing.
3. Label hanging folders at the front so that all corresponding file folders follow the label.
4. Consider labeling file folders on the outside so that the contents follow the label.
5. Arrange papers in any file folder with the most recent on top, since you are likely to refer to a paper on a current matter.
6. Attach papers to a file folder so that they do not fall out when you retrieve it. Use binder clips at the bottom of the paperwork so that you can leaf through papers without detaching them. Rotate binder clips so that they do not take up too much room in your file drawer.

TIP

File as you go.

7. For files that have a shelf life, mark them with a date on which the contents can be shredded and recycled.

8. Staple papers that belong together in a file; paper clips slip off.

See 5.3   Setting up a Filing System

See 5.4   Categorizing Your Files

5.6 Evaluating Your Filing System

I've been in business for awhile now, and my filing system is in a shambles. I don't know where to file particular items, and worse, I can't find important papers all too often. How do I sort this mess?

Filing paperwork related to your practice takes time. That's a fact. Yet you cannot set aside this task for a later time. You will never catch up. Worse, inefficiency in dealing with business papers keeps you from generating the best kind of papers: drawings.

To evaluate your current filing system, ask yourself how often the following statements, adapted from *The Organized Executive,* by Stephanie Winston, pertain to it.

TEN ATTRIBUTES OF AN EFFICIENT FILING SYSTEM

1. You can find any paper in your desk files within 3 minutes.
2. Your staff can find any paper in the office files within 5 minutes.
3. You file research material and supporting data with the final project, not in separate files.
4. You discard outdated papers no more than 2 years after needing or using them.
5. You label your file folders with descriptive labels.
6. You do not fill your files with unnecessary duplicate copies of papers.

7. You keep a half hour's worth or less of papers in your "to file" box.

8. You organize your papers in broad categories without too many subcategories so that similar papers are kept together.

9. You make file labels that are easy to read by using a large font on your computer or by hand lettering with block lettering.

10. You leave enough room in each file drawer so that papers are not wedged in among one another.

See 5.3   Setting up a Filing System
See 5.4   Categorizing Your Files
See 5.5   Keeping a Filing System
See 5.9   Avoiding Excess Copies

5 PAPER: FILES

Holding Onto Tax Records

With limited filing space, I need to get rid of some papers. How long must I hold onto tax records?

Hold onto tax records for a minimum of 3 years from the date of filing your tax return.

See 4.23 Reporting and Paying Taxes

5.8 Using a Project Notebook

In the firm where I used to work, we used project notebooks to keep pertinent information about a project. Now that I am on my own, is this the most efficient way to store paperwork?

Whether or not to use project notebooks depends on the size of your practice. If a number of staffers need to refer to the papers pertaining to a project, a project notebook is a handy way to organize those papers to tell the story of the project. If you are a sole practitioner, consider working your projects out of a conveniently located file drawer, using appropriately labeled manila folders. This keeps all materials related to a project in one place.

PAPER: FILES

Avoiding Excess Copies

How can I rid my office of excess copies?

Extra copies of papers take up room in file drawers, especially if they are part of a multipaged document. If a document is pertinent to two file folders in your filing system, place a note in one of them that states where the important document is stored.

Before putting a piece of paper into a file to take up space, consider whether the information exists elsewhere, whether the information could be gotten elsewhere, and most important, whether it would really matter if the information were lost.

Using Project Numbers

We used project numbers in the firms for which I worked. They seemed so impersonal. Do I need to use them in my practice? Why can't I simply use the client's name to identify a project? If I do use project numbers, how do I determine them?

Project numbers are particularly impersonal in residential architecture practice, where you work with clients on a very personal level to design their houses. While it is certainly feasible to refer to your projects by your clients' names, project numbers do serve a practical purpose.

Use project numbers as accounting codes to track long-distance telephone calls. Organize your paper and computer files numerically with project numbers. Project numbers, if determined sequentially, remind you of which projects came first, allowing you to work on them in order. Best of all, project numbers help you differentiate between projects for repeat clients.

TIP

If you plan to use project numbers as accounting codes for long-distance telephone calls, ask your long-distance provider how many digits you can use to make up a code number.

Project numbers generally combine the last two digits of the year that the project was commissioned and two or three digits that tell of its place in your line-up of projects, for example, 1001 for the first project in the year 2010. Use two digits if you expect to have between 1 and 99 projects in a given year and three digits if you expect to have between 1 and 999 projects in a year.

See 4.14 Signing up for Telephone Accounting Codes
See 5.3   Setting up a Filing System

TIP

Make up project numbers for general office functions such as literature requests, marketing calls, supply orders, etc.

PAPER: FILES

Sorting Piles of Paper

Piles and piles of paper of all kinds have accumulated all over my office. I know that I probably should be filing as I go, but what can I do right now to begin organizing my papers quickly?

If you do not have time to file papers where they belong, at least sort them. The following system works for piles of paper that will not fit into a single manila folder.

SIX STEPS TO SORTING PILES OF PAPER

1. Clear a work surface.
2. Make "name cards" for the categories in which you expect to file the papers by folding index cards in half crosswise and labeling them.
3. Stand the name cards on your work surface.
4. Sort papers, making additional name cards as they occur to you.
5. Once you have completed sorting the papers, put rubber bands around the piles of sorted papers and stand the name cards on top of the piles or secure them to the piles with the rubber bands.
6. Add to the neat piles of papers as more come in, and file the papers where they belong when you get a moment.

See 5.4 Categorizing Your Files

> **MUSING**
>
> ▼
>
> **Stuff sorted into teetering piles is called *columnar chaos*.**

PAPER: STATIONERY

Choosing Stationery

Do I have to use traditional business stationery for my correspondence?

Select or design letterhead that both reflects the image of your firm and meets the expectations of your clientele. Indeed, a residential architect's stationery would, and probably should, look different from stationery of an architect who designs office buildings or hospitals. Clients expect architects to be creative, so your letterhead probably can deviate from the norm a little without it casting a bad light on your firm.

Use your letterhead for correspondence other than letters, such as transmittals and statements of services. Use it as the basis for designing standardized office forms. Consider using your slogan on your letterhead.

See 1.12 Writing a Slogan
See 5.14 Using Standardized Forms
See Appendix B
See Appendix C

TIP

Deeply or brightly colored envelopes
stand out in a pile of softly colored mail.
If you opt for them, use white mailing
labels to ensure legible addresses.

Over the years, I have received a variety of letterheads designed by architects, from a blurry photocopy on bond, to a unique rubber stamp on writing paper, to exquisite two-tone type on 100 percent cotton paper. One architect screened his name in a pale color under the body of his letter, almost as if to repeat it subliminally.

When I opened my practice, I designed my own letterhead using the limited capabilities of my computer's word processing program. By printing my own letterhead, I cut down on costs and left open the opportunity to adjust my design as I used the letterhead on a daily basis.

Subsequently, I used the letterhead as the basis for the design of my business-size envelope, my mailing labels, my business card, and the postcards that I use from time to time. Ultimately, it became the basis for the several standardized forms I use to keep track of everything from outgoing mail to stationery orders to telephone conversations with clients.

PAPER: STATIONERY

Stocking Stationery

I am setting up a business for the first time and need to stock my stationery cabinet. What items should I choose?

To stock your cabinet with the stationery you need for all occasions, choose the following.

ITEMS IN A WELL-STOCKED STATIONERY CABINET

▼ Letterhead

Use this for letters, memoranda, letters of transmittal, and monthly statements of services rendered.

▼ Office forms

Use your letterhead as the base for the following fill-in-the-blank forms:

Automobile mileage record
Billable hours tally sheet
Field reports
General contractors' client interview notes
Individual expenses record
Meeting notes
Prospective client interview notes
Stationery and supplies order
Telephone conversation record
Telephone call log

▼ Cards

Have on hand the following types of cards:

Blank cards to use for thank-you notes, brief messages, and other personal correspondence

Postcards to use for quick messages and to request product literature

Holiday cards to thank clients for their patronage, employees for their work, and consultants and vendors for their service

▼ Brochures

Keep these brochures on hand to mail out immediately after an inquiry about your services:

Architecture, to explain your projects and services

Design counseling, to explain the terms of this unique service, if you offer it

▼ Envelopes

Keep a variety of envelopes handy to accommodate the different types of mail you send:

No.10 Business-size envelopes

Size A envelopes for invitation-size blank cards

9 × 12 inch envelopes for $8^{1}/_{2}$ × 11 inch sheets and small batches of drawings

Priority and Express Mail envelopes for urgent papers and larger batches of drawings

▼ Labels

Labels printed with your return address to get mail out faster

See 5.14 Using Standardized Forms
See Appendix B
See Appendix C

TIP

Preprint a page of labels for each client to get correspondence, statements of services rendered, and drawings in the mail more quickly.

Using Standardized Forms

I have a lot of writing pads started with all kinds of information on them. How can I visually distinguish the topics of my scribblings and keep track of them?

Writing on anything at hand, with the intent to copy the information later where it belongs, just wastes time. Write down information only once.

To keep better notes, use standardized forms. Design fill-in-the-blank forms on your letterhead that provide space for note taking on any repetitive activity in your practice. Devise a fill-in-the-blank format to prompt you for vital information when you use them.

An example of a standardized form is a telephone conversation record form. Blank spaces prompt you to fill in pertinent information such as the party's name, the telephone number, and the date. A spot to jot down the time span of the conversation helps you keep track of your billable hours.

Develop other forms for meeting notes, site visits, and interviews with prospective clients. Keep records of stationery and drafting supplies orders on standardized forms as well. Consider color coding all or some of your forms. Store completed forms in their designated three-ring binders.

See 5.12   Choosing Stationery
See 5.13   Stocking Stationery
See 5.17   Writing Correspondence
See Appendix B
See Appendix C

5 PAPER: CORRESPONDENCE

5.15 Using Correspondence

I spend a lot of time corresponding with the various players in my architectural practice. How can I cut down on writing time and still get the results I want?

First, decide whether correspondence is appropriate in a given situation. If a telephone call will move things along, make one. If a face-to-face meeting will work better, schedule one. If e-mail will forward the information, use it.

Remember, though, if the subject matter of that telephone call or meeting becomes an issue of debate, you will have nothing more than your notes and your memory to plead your case.

E-mail is essentially an electronic postcard. Therefore, use correspondence to announce, to confirm, to clarify, to commit to, to renege on, and to remind people about important issues pertaining to your practice.

See 5.17 Writing Correspondence

TIP

For a short and quick response to a piece
of incoming correspondence, jot your
reply on the original, make a photocopy
of it, and send it back to the sender.

Creating a Paper Trail

There are many kinds of papers that I deal with in the running of my practice. What about the paperwork that I generate and send to my clients? How much of a paper trail should I create for clients?

The telephone and e-mail cut down on the amount of paperwork you generate with respect to clients. Still, create enough of a paper trail to serve as a diary of your dealings with clients with respect to their projects. If issues arise surrounding your handling of a particular matter, a letter defends you better than your hazy recollection of a particular telephone conversation.

Concerns about inundating your clients with too much paperwork are unfounded: Let them decide whether or not to read information you send. At least you will have protected yourself by writing about critical issues surrounding a project.

Writing Correspondence

How do I write correspondence efficiently?

Architects generate more legitimate paperwork than they receive: drawings, specifications, agreements, letters, transmittals, memoranda, monthly statements, etc. The longer you are in business, the easier it becomes to compose the different forms of correspondence needed to practice architecture. Establishing standard formats for your correspondence takes time, though.

Preprinted forms for common types of correspondence sent by architects are available. Store-bought forms for memoranda and transmittals often feature instant duplicates.

Consider designing your own forms on the computer by making templates that incorporate your letterhead into the design of memoranda, transmittals, and even your monthly statements. Either print these templates to fill in by hand as needed, or use them to write correspondence on the computer.

How you actually use the forms depends on the image of your firm. If handwritten forms will not offend your clients' sensibilities, use them. If your clients expect the utmost in professionalism, generate your correspondence on the computer. Either method is an efficient way to write correspondence.

Naturally, once you have written any one of the forms of correspondence on the computer, you can simply edit the next time you need a similar article.

See 1.11 Creating an Image for Your Firm
See 5.14 Using Standardized Forms
See 5.15 Using Correspondence

 # Handling Mail

Are there any tips for handling incoming mail?

Handling incoming mail can be a time-consuming prospect, particularly if you let it pile up to be dealt with at a later time. The pile grows quickly because of the variety of items that constitute incoming mail. To handle your mail, try *reading* it.

READING YOUR MAIL

▼ R is for respond

Answer correspondence and fill in informational requests when they come in. If a telephone call or a quick e-mail message will suffice as a response, make or send one.

▼ E is for examine

Consider offers for bank loans, credit cards, and subscriptions. Leaf through professional journals, magazines, or books to look for information that may be pertinent to your practice or projects.

▼ A is for assign

Delegate the handling of particular mail items to your staff.

▼ D is for delay

Set aside mail that you cannot examine or assign or to which you cannot respond immediately.

MUSING

Paper is the enemy.

▼ I is for insert

File product literature and samples in project files or in your product library. File licenses, registrations, and insurance policies in their designated folders. Replace outdated code pages with revisions.

▼ N is for note

Record payments from clients in your bank book. List invoices on your payment sheet. Mark appointments on your calendar.

▼ G is for grind

Shred, tear, crumple, and recycle unwanted mail.

See 5.19 Stopping Junk Mail

TIP

Open your daily mail with your paper shredder or recycling bin nearby. This way, you handle unwanted mail only once, sending it out as soon as it comes in.

Stopping Junk Mail

A good portion of the mail with which I am deluged on a daily basis is junk mail. How can I stop it?

To stop junk mail, ask the Direct Marketing Association to add your name to its "delete list," which is distributed to its members. Write to it at

Mail Preference Service
Direct Marketing Association
P.O. Box 9008
Farmingdale, NY 11735-9008

To stop credit card offers specifically, send your full name and current address to

Consumer Opt-out Service
TRW Inc.
P.O. Box 919
Allen, TX 75002

or call 800-353-0809.

See 5.18 Handling Mail

PAPER: BOOKS

Making Books Part of a Collection

As a student and intern architect, I amassed a collection of books that needs to be organized into my reference library. How do I organize my books simply?

TIP

▼

Find bargains on architecture books at used bookstores near colleges and universities.

You can organize your books in a logical manner without turning to the Dewey decimal system. Simply organize your books according to the categories with which you identify them. This should be easy, since your books most likely fall into broad categories pertinent to your work. Shelve your books according to these categories. Arrange the categories alphabetically or with similar categories adjacent to one another. Once the books are shelved, alphabetize them by author and title if you like, although a quick scan of any category probably will reveal the title you are after. As you organize your books, make an inventory of them according to category. Sort books by category on your computer to group like titles with one another.

When I organized my pile of books into a reference library for my residential practice, I devised four-letter abbreviations for the categories that comprise it. My collection of books is organized by categories that I associate with my work. Here are some examples of the categories:

AMER   American architecture
ASIA   Asian architecture
BUSI   Business
CITY   Urban planning
COMP   Computers
EURO   European architecture
FURN   Furniture
GARD   Gardening and landscaping
HIST   Architectural history
INTD   Interior design
MODE   Modern architecture
PERS   Individual architects
PROF   The profession
TECH   Technical
THEO   Architectural theory
TYPE   Building types

 # Managing Periodicals

I subscribe to several trade journals and lots of magazines, which I use as practice guides, product resources, and design barometers for my architectural practice. How do I manage my periodicals without saving them all or recycling them all?

Periodicals fall into three categories: those you want to keep, those you want to discard, and those you want to keep in part.

Shelve trade journals with your other reference books. Consider purchasing an index that helps you research topics of interest. As space runs out, decide how to handle older journals; get rid of them or keep parts of them.

To keep parts of periodicals permanently for their informational value or design inspiration, tear them up and save them in three-ring binders. Include the covers of the magazines to identify the source of the articles. Also keep the lists of resources that go with the articles if you want to specify building products at some time in the future.

To keep parts of periodicals for a short time, until you get to read the articles, tear them out and store them in a folder marked "to read." This method is especially helpful in keeping down the accumulation of newspapers and magazines.

See 3.14 Getting Organized

To illustrate their goals for new houses or residential additions, my clients often show me pages torn from the latest magazines. Their handfuls of clippings are no match to the arsenal of clippings I've been saving since before opening my practice. Selecting articles to save is a purely subjective process: I save what I like. Such articles exhibit my design sensibilities and usually appeal to the clients I attract. But why save clippings from periodicals when styles change and new trends are constantly emerging? Good ideas never go out of style. I've referred to clippings from as far back as 10 years.

PHOTOGRAPHS AND SUCH

Organizing Negatives, Photographs, and Slides

What do I do with my piles of negatives, photographs, and slides?

Use plastic sleeves made for three-ring binders to organize your negatives, photographs, and slides. First and foremost, they protect them from fingerprints. The $8^1/2 \times 11$ inch sheets are easier to handle than the individual pieces.

These protectors have an advantage over using boxes or cases for storing negatives, photographs, and slides: It is easier and quicker to find particular items by leafing through the photograph protectors or by holding the negatives and slide protectors up to the light or over a light board. File the sleeves in manila folders in your file drawers, in project notebooks, or in a three-ring binder designated for pictures.

MY FAVORITE STUFF

▼

Here's a list of eight items that have made my professional life a lot easier. Although I had to wait to purchase or subscribe to some of them because of financial considerations, I couldn't work without them now.

1. THREE-RING BINDER ◆ Three-ring binders are my preferred way to hold just about everything in my office because they can be stored on shelves. I use three-ring binders to hold my checkbook and checking account register, project information, telephone conversation records, stationery and supply order forms, book orders, and magazine clippings. Filled with plastic sleeves, they can be used to store computer disks, photographs, slides, and negatives.

2. SHREDDER ◆ An avid recycler, I toss anything from blank checks to credit card applications into my recycling bin. Aware that I should not let proprietary information about me or my clients go out to the curb, I shred it.

3. POSTAL SCALE ◆ I used to spend an inordinate amount of time waiting on line at the post office to have a letter or a package of drawings weighed. Now I have on hand a 5-lb scale and a stockpile of stamps to take care of any outgoing mail. My postal carrier takes my mail to the post office for me, saving me the trip.

4. MOUSE PAD WITH BUILT-IN CALCULATOR ◆ Although many computers have an on-screen calculator, I use a mousepad with a built-in calculator when I am calculating monthly statements of services rendered and reimbursables. It is handy to have a calculator near the computer at all times.

MY FAVORITE STUFF (continued)

5. SCANNER ◆ My scanner takes the place of a copy machine and a facsimile machine in my office, which is cramped for space. Great for single copies of a document at odd hours, it has saved me many trips to the copy center. As a facsimile machine, it is invaluable.

6. SPEAKER PHONE ◆ Although I try not to speak to my clients, or anybody else for that matter, on a speaker phone, I use it when I am put on hold by a client or a customer service representative. While I wait for the other party to pick up again, I continue to work.

7. CALLER ID ◆ By displaying the name and telephone number of the caller on its panel, the caller ID box allows me to answer calls from clients while avoiding unwanted sales calls. This is especially important during the construction phase of a project, when clients need immediate answers from me about things taking place in the field.

8. VOICE MAIL ◆ Voice mail is more useful than an answering machine. It answers a call while I am on the phone and saves messages that I want to listen to again. With it, I can record an extended absence greeting to be played when I'm out of the office for a few days, for example, at a convention.

CONCLUSION

The biggest problem in the world
Could have been solved when it was small.

   —Witter Bynner
    The Way of Life
    According to Lao-tzu

If it does nothing else, *The Architect's Business Problem Solver* demonstrates that the day-to-day problems that arise in architectural practice take many forms. In doing so, it bears witness to the complex and contradictory nature of architectural practice. In their exposé of best-run American companies, *In Search of Excellence*, Thomas J. Peters and Robert H. Waterman, Jr., note (1982: xxi): "If there is one striking feature of the excellent companies, it is the ability to manage ambiguity and paradox."

This disparate collection of problems and solutions intends to bolster you with essential information about a variety of topics in the same way architectural standards books arm you with vital information about a variety of building assemblies. While these books cannot design entire buildings for you, they can provide details for building parts to help you put a building together bit by bit. *The Architect's Business Problem Solver* cannot run your practices for you. Rather, it offers detailed business strategies from which to pick and choose to advance your practices bit by bit.

Hopefully, having this book as a handy reference on your desk will quell the panic, ease the frustration, and shed light on the uncertainty that threatens practice. Building blocks can be stacked into place. People can be reasoned with. Time constraints can be loosened. Money matters can be figured out. And stuff can be sorted out.

Solving Any Problem

Is there one solution that might apply to any problem that arises in the day-to-day running of my architectural practice?

All the solutions in *The Architect's Business Problem Solver* are worded to promote action. While there are many dos, there are no don'ts. There is one, and only one, don't to which I ascribe. It makes up the one solution that might apply to any problem you encounter in the day-to-day running of your practice. A valuable piece of advice offered repeatedly by my father when I was faced with a problem, it is the only rule offered in this book.

FIRST RULE IN SOLVING ANY PROBLEM

Don't overreact.

AFTERWORD

If you have built castles in the air,
Your work need not be lost;
That is where they should be.
Now put the foundations under them.

—Henry David Thoreau

As it turns out, many storms lay ahead of me when I embarked on my adventure in sole practitionership. Not seeded by my own doing, these storms were brewed from an invisible source: the absence of experience. Seeking any port in a storm, I looked to anyone and everyone to protect me from these hailstorms of problems. By imploring others for help, even if they were authors by way of the pages in their books, I did not travel alone.

We gain experience through experiences shared by others. We gain experience by devising moves for our own solutions, though awkward and redundant at times. We gain experience by taking advantage of opportunities. And problems? They are merely opportunities that come looking for us. While we might occasionally skirt around them, we usually get out of them by going through them. And it is with this first step, which always seems like a giant one, that we decidedly, decisively take action.

If you have taken some of the tips, used some of the tactics, and employed some of the techniques offered in this book, perhaps you have come to agree with me that it is action that ensures protection from the precipitation that threatens practice. We change from this to that. We move from here to there. Action encourages advancement. Advancement engenders success.

But how do we continue to advance beyond what *The Architects Business Problem Solver* tells us? I am working on my own solution to that problem right now. Indeed, I have not devised the definitive step-by-step strategy for it yet. However, I have begun to anticipate how I may propel my practice forward.

As I find new resources, I will look to them for solutions to the problems that arise in practice. I anticipate that my newly acquired books will help me in the same way that my trusty standbys have helped me over the past ten years. I anticipate finding more new information and books through organizations, government agencies, and companies catering to my needs in business and specifically to my needs in the field of architecture.

Much of my focus will remain on cultivating mutually beneficial working relationships with the people of practice, one of the most rewarding aspects of my practice so far. I anticipate that, like in the past, as I befriend clients, employees, consultants, contractors, and the like, they will become invaluable sounding boards for the strategies I devise to combat the issues that surround me. Successfully communicating with these individuals will continue to be a major goal.

I anticipate that technology will play a larger role in my practice as I rely more on my home computer to help me sort out, sift through, and straighten up some of the facts and figures that flood my practice. And I look forward with eager anticipation to the informational journeys that the Internet will surely afford me. For me, much of the first decade of my practice was about keeping my head above water. I anticipate that the second decade and beyond will be about sailing the distance. Although I have yet to determine where my practice and I will ultimately end up, I have logged in the next ports of call, some of them old, some of them new. I anticipate that my visits to them will expose me to situations that will inspire me to continue to guide my practice in the right direction. Perhaps they will inspire you too.

APPENDIX

Resources

This disparate selection of books, companies, government agencies, organizations, periodicals, and Websites makes up the resources that I tend to consult for solutions to problems that are not addressed in *The Architect's Business Problem Solver*. These resources make up a handful of what I believe will be important resources for advancing my architecture practice in the near future. Consider looking at them first for help outside *The Architect's Business Problem Solver*.

Books

The books listed below, from my own library, are those that I will consult when faced with new challenges in my practice. Some are recent acquisitions waiting to be read from cover to cover. Others are tried and true favorites that I have used over and over again and referred to often throughout this book. They are loosely organized by broad subjects.

PRACTICE THEORY

The first step to being *in* practice is to ask ourselves: what *is* practice? Each of the following four books attempts to answer that question for us.

Cramer, James P. 1994. *Design Plus Enterprise: Seeking a New Reality in Architecture.* Washington, DC: AIA Press.

> Dedicated in part to taking action, which is of course the whole point behind *The Architect's Business Problem Solver, Design Plus Enterprise* looks at opportunities in the field of architecture. Read it to shape your own future in the field.

Cuff, Dana. 1991. *Architecture: The Story of Practice.* Cambridge, Mass.: MIT Press.

> If the how-to guides on running an architectural firm are the brawn behind *The Architect's Business Problem Solver,* then *Architecture: The Story of Practice* is the brains. Cuff's portrayal of the field of architecture caused me to ask myself the single most important question that generated this book: What can I do to make the day-to-day practice of architecture a little easier?

Gutman, Robert. 1988. *Architectural Practice: A Critical View.* New York: Princeton Architectural Press.

> In *Architectural Practice,* Gutman describes trends in architecture to help you determine where to focus your efforts.

Lewis, Roger K. 1985. *Architect? A Candid Guide to the Profession.* Cambridge, Mass.: MIT Press.

> Although directed mainly to readers thinking about entering the field of architecture, *Architect?* deserves praise for its broad-stroke coverage of the field of architecture. Part III, Being an Architect, presents an overview of the architectural profession, covering topics such as the building process and the architect's role, how architects work, how architects get work, and architects' clients. Its often humorous characterization of architects as types will help you identify and analyze your professional persona.

HOW-TO

Each of the books listed below has its individual strengths. Combined, these books make up a powerful arsenal for attacking the challenges of starting and operating your architectural practice.

Franklin, James R. 1990. *Current Practices in Small Firm Management: An Architect's Notebook.* Washington: American Institute of Architects.

> Use this book in conjunction with *The Architect's Handbook of Professional Practice* for The American Institute of Architects' approach to running an architectural firm.

Haviland, David. 1988. *The Architect's Handbook of Professional Practice,* 11th ed. Washington: American Institute of Architects.

> *The Architect's Handbook of Professional Practice* is The American Institute of Architects' official guide to starting and operating your own architectural firm. The biggest and most expensive of the how-to guides recommended here, it includes copies of and commentaries on AIA documents that you can use to define the terms by which you will work with the people involved in architecture projects.

Kaderlan, Norman. 1991. *Designing Your Practice.* New York: McGraw-Hill.

> Along with *How to Start and Operate Your Own Design Firm* and *Staying Small Successfully, Designing Your Practice* gives strength to the practical backbone of *The Architect's Business Problem Solver.* Read this quintessential how-to guide from cover to cover.

Knackstedt, Mary V. 1988. *The Interior Design Business Handbook: A Complete Guide to Profitability.* New York: Whitney Library of Design.

Written from the perspective of an interior designer, this book is an interesting contrast to the how-to guides for architects. Like these other how-to books, *The Interior Design Business Handbook* offers advice on topics such as public relations, advertising, setting fees, and managing the office. Read its sage advice about determining the location of your business as it relates to the image of your firm.

Morgan, Jim. 1998. *Management for the Small Design Firm: Handling Your Practice, Personnel, Finances and Projects.* New York: Whitney Library of Design.

Management for the Small Design Firm effectively explicates management theory for the small design firm. Review Morgan's list of financial management programs for the computer if you are considering a purchase. Over half of the book is devoted to Design-Practice Dialogues, which are telling case studies of 15 design firms.

Pressman, Andy. 1997. *Professional Practice 101: A Compendium of Business and Management Strategies in Architecture.* New York: John Wiley & Sons.

In *Professional Practice 101*, Pressman observes that a certain amount of practical knowledge is required to achieve success in the real world. He sets out to impart such knowledge to you with selections on practice-related issues written by expert guest authors. This format allows you to read the book in installments as certain issues arise in your practice.

Rubeling, Albert W., Jr. 1994. *How to Start and Operate Your Own Design Firm.* New York: McGraw-Hill.

Rubeling's *How to Start and Operate Your Own Design Firm* is one of three books that help form the practical backbone of *The Architect's Business Problem Solver*. The quintessential how-to guide, read it along with *Designing Your Practice* and *Staying Small Successfully* when you have the time.

Stasiowski, Frank A. 1994. *Starting a New Design Firm, or Risking It All.* New York: John Wiley & Sons.

In *Starting a New Design Firm,* Stasiowski boils the launching of a practice into four discreet parts. Build one upon the other to get your own practice going. He raises an interesting point about defining the culture of your practice in addition to writing a mission statement and developing a business plan.

Stasiowski, Frank A. 1991. *Staying Small Successfully: A Guide for Architects, Engineers and Design Professionals.* New York: John Wiley & Sons.

Stasiowski's book is one of a trio of books that give a stable base to *The Architect's Business Problem Solver*. Use it along with *Designing Your Practice* and *How to Start and Operate Your Own Design Firm.*

CLIENT RELATIONS

Use these books learn how to deal with clients and more.

Baker, John Milnes, AIA. 1988. *How to Build a House with an Architect.* New York: Harper & Row.

If you can find a copy of this out-of-print book, lend it to prospective and actual clients of residential design. A primer for the first-time user of architectural services, *How to Build a House with an Architect* explains the architect's role, the client's role and the contractor's role in designing and building a house. An invaluable section broaches the topic of architect's fees for you.

Harrigan, John E., and Paul R. Neel. 1996. *The Executive Architect: Transforming Designers into Leaders.* New York: John Wiley & Sons.

The Executive Architect emphasizes the client side of professional practice. Insights into practice offered by professionals in the building industry contribute to the especially helpful chapters on client relations and working with clients.

Kliment, Stephen A. 1998. *Writing for Design Professionals: A Guide to Writing Successful Proposals, Letters, Brochures, Portfolios, Reports, Presentations, and Job Applications.* New York: W.W. Norton.

In his introduction to *Writing for Design Professionals,* Kliment makes a case for why writing matters and then supports it with the rest of his book. Besides discussing techniques for the usual writing assignments that architects encounter, such as letters, proposals, brochures, etc., he offers timely advice on writing e-mail and copy for Websites.

Pressman, Andy. 1995. *The Fountainheadache: The Politics of Architect-Client Relations.* New York: John Wiley & Sons.

The Fountainheadache stresses the importance of the architect and client relationship in successful architecture projects. Combining stories from famous architects with accounts of his own fledgling practice, Pressman offers invaluable advice on those all-important relationships in your professional life.

TIME MANAGEMENT

Consider adding a time management book like the following to your practice library. Books on time management are very popular. Select one that suits you and add it to your practice library. Consider the one below.

Winston, Stephanie. 1983. *The Organized Executive*. New York: Warner Books.

> Several of the techniques offered throughout *The Architect's Business Problem Solver* are adapted from *The Organized Executive*. In her book, Winston tells you how to conduct your professional life in order to achieve maximum productivity in a way that is consistent with your long term goals.

MONEY MANAGEMENT

These two books give you a business-based view and an architecture-based view, respectively, of accounting and other financial concerns.

Dixon, Robert L. 1982. *The McGraw-Hill 36-Hour Accounting Course*. New York: McGraw-Hill.

> Basic tenets are covered in *The McGraw-Hill 36-Hour Accounting Course* for business owners who seek a working knowledge of accounting. The abbreviated format is in keeping with the philosophy of *The Architect's Business Problem Solver* — to learn techniques and implement them quickly.

Getz, Lowell. 1997. *An Architect's Guide to Financial Management*. Washington, DC: AIA Press.

As its title implies, *An Architect's Guide to Financial Management* concerns itself with all aspects of the financial health of your architectural firm. Highlights include discussions of determining overhead, invoicing and collecting fees, and managing cash. Consult it if you are considering the advantages of a computerized accounting system.

BUSINESS SKILLS

Read the following book before or instead of pursuing a degree in business to complement your degree in architecture.

Collins, Eliza G.C. and Mary Anne Devanna. 1990. *The Portable MBA*. New York: John Wiley & Sons.

If you ever wished you had the time, money, and energy to work toward a Master of Business Administration degree to acquire the business acumen that you need to run your firm better, read *The Portable MBA* to discover which skills you are missing.

OFFICE SKILLS

Like the how-to guides listed above, these handbooks offer invaluable information for managing some of the prosaic aspects of your practice.

Houghton Mifflin. 1984. *The Professional Secretary's Handbook*. New York: Houghton Mifflin.

Particularly helpful to the sole practitioner who finds him- or herself in charge of all tasks, *The Professional Secretary's Handbook* offers advice on basic secretarial skills that might not be included in your repertoire. Follow these examples to avoid appearing amateurish in your handling of the prosaic aspects of business.

While any secretarial handbook would be a welcome addition to your library, this particular book includes chapters that cover business English, the dos and don'ts of copying, handling conventional and electronic mail, generating business documents, and the ins and outs of telecommunication.

Society of Design Administration. 1999. *Handbook of Design Office Administration.* New York: John Wiley & Sons.

If you are a sole practitioner, read this book. If you employ someone to run your office, read this book and then give it to him or her. *The Handbook of Design Office Administration* looks at the administrative side of architecture practice in depth. Practical matters such as accounting, travel arrangements, and insurance are covered in a book to be kept within arm's reach. A chapter on human resources reviews government compliance programs and employee benefits. As an added bonus, the book comes with a computer disk.

Stevens, Mark. 1988. *The Macmillan Small Business Handbook.* New York: Macmillan.

A basic business handbook like *The Macmillan Small Business Handbook* is an important reference if you are a business owner who needs to familiarize yourself with standard practices in the business world at large.

Organizations and Companies

The companies, government agencies, and organizations listed below are mentioned throughout *The Architect's Business Problem Solver*. The majority of them are sources to which I will turn for solutions to new problems that are sure to arise in my practice.

American Institute of Architects (AIA)
1735 New York Avenue, NW
Washington, DC 20006

Telephone number: 202-626-7300
Website address: www.aiaonline.com or www.e-architect.com
Practice information: 202-626-7364
Practice Website address: www.e-architect.com/pia/practman
Library: 202-626-7493

When faced with any question about architecture, look first to The American Institute of Architects (AIA). The AIA offers a wealth of information to architects involved in a variety of disparate endeavors, regardless of whether they are members or not. Going one step further than merely offering information about running an architecture practice, the AIA sponsors special programs for its members' enrollment, programs like health and life insurance for individuals and business owners.

The AIA library is a great resource for research. Some of its materials are available to borrow under conditions based on membership.

Professional Interest Areas (PIAs) meet the specialized needs of AIA members. For example, the Practice Management PIA offers its subscribers practice-related information in mailings sent out throughout the year. Such mailings are good sources for learning about AIA-sponsored conferences, seminars, and workshops that deal with practice. The AIA's Website offers information on practice-related issues to anyone with access to the internet. Be aware that select areas of AIA On-line are accessible to AIA members only.

Direct Marketing Association
Mail Preference Service
P.O. Box 9008
Farmingdale, NY 11735-9008

To stop junk mail, ask the Direct Marketing Association to add your name to its "delete list," which is distributed to its members.

Guidelines
Box 456
Orinda, CA 94563

Telephone number: 800-634-7779
Facsimile Number: 925-299-0181

Guidelines is a small architectural publishing firm that prepares extremely useful and timely manuals, checklists, training materials, and management guides for architects.

In addition to offering the study-at-home course on Design Counseling that is mentioned several times in this book, Guidelines offers a variety of publications aimed at helping you to run your business and your projects more efficiently.

A monthly newsletter is available that offers articles on the various aspects of running an architecture practice.

Internal Revenue Service (IRS)
Live tax help: 800-829-1040 (most areas)
Recorded tax information: 800-829-4477 (most areas)

Forms and publications: 800-829-3676

Forms and instructions by facsimile: 703-368-9694

Website address: www.irs.ustreas.gov

> For information about taxes direct from the source, contact the Internal Revenue Service. General information on many topics is available on recorded messages that you can access by telephone. Live representatives answer your telephone calls about questions that are not addressed in the recorded messages. Despite initial trepidation about actually talking to the IRS, I have found the representatives to be helpful and knowledgeable in answering specific questions about my particular tax situation.

TRW, Inc.

Consumer Opt-Out Service

P.O. Box 919

Allen, TX 75002

Telephone number: 800-353-0809

> To stop credit card offers, send your full name and current address to the Consumer Opt-Out Service at TRW, Inc.

U.S. Small Business Administration (SBA)

Office of Marketing and Customer Service

409 Third Street, SW, Suite 7600

Washington, DC 20416

Telephone number: 202-205-6744

Facsimile number: 202-205-6913

Answers to small business questions: 800-UASKBA

Website address: www.sba.gov

> When faced with any question about small business, look first to the U.S. Small Business Administration (SBA). The

SBA offers a wealth of information about starting and running a small business. It offers publications and sponsors programs and loans. Its publications expand on many of the topics that are touched on in *The Architect's Business Problem Solver.* Many of these publications are available on the SBA Website, along with information about special programs run by the SBA.

Periodicals

The periodicals listed below regularly include articles about practice-related issues. Subscribing to one will keep you abreast of architectural events as they occur and concerns as they arise across the country.

AIArchitect
The American Institute of Architects
1735 New York Avenue, NW
Washington, DC 20006-5292

Subscription: 202-626-7365

The official newspaper of The American Institute of Architects, *AIArchitect* disseminates information on a wide variety of topics on a monthly basis. Articles on topics ranging from design-related issues to practice matters allow you to keep in touch with the goings on in the field of architecture from the perspective of the AIA.

AIArchitect is available on the internet.
Website address: www.e-architect.com/news/news.asp

Architectural Record

P.O. Box 564

Hightstown, NJ 08520-9885

Subscription: 888-867-6395

> Monthly articles on a wide variety of topics pertaining to the field of architecture comprise *Architectural Record*. Columns on practice matters are included regularly. A subscription to *Architectural Record* is included with membership in its affiliate, The American Institute of Architects.
>
> Portions of *Architectural Record* are available on the internet.
>
> Website address: www.archrecord.com

Architecture

P.O. Box 2063

Marion, OH 43306-2163

Subscription: 800-745-8922

> *Architecture*, a monthly publication that is independent from any architectural organization, offers feature articles on a wide variety of topics pertaining to the field of architecture, including practice matters.
>
> Portions of *Architecture* are available on the internet.
>
> Website address: www.architecturemag.com

Websites

Use the four Websites listed below as starting points for conducting research on the internet. Unlike the Websites of the companies, government agencies, and organizations listed above, which reflect the missions of those organizations, the Websites listed below are shaped more directly by their creators' outlooks on architecture. Idiosyncratic perspectives are apparent from the topics of feature articles included on these sites. First and foremost, use these Websites to connect to those sites that will lead you to the information you seek. For the most part, they lead to well-known and reputable companies, organizations, etc.

Architectstore.com
Website address: www.architectstore.com

> Besides being a Website that sells books through a link with the on-line bookstore *Amazon.com, Architectstore.com* offers links to other Websites on the internet with information about architecture.

Cyburbia.org
Website address: cyburbia.ap.buffalo.edu

> Hosted by the University of Buffalo School of Architecture and Planning, Cyburbia.org is a Website designed and updated by a former planning student. Like some of the other architecture Websites listed here, it offers links to other Websites with information about the field of architecture.

Plan net.com
Website address: www.plannet.com

> Plan net.com is a Website that offers links to Websites on the internet with information on architecture.

Studyweb.com
Website address: www.studyweb.com/architecture

Although predominantly a research tool for school-age students completing class assignments, Studyweb.com is a solid starting point to begin research about many aspects of the field of architecture, from architecture schools and programs to books, magazines, and publications to organizations. Besides being a launching pad for research about these practical aspects of the field, Studyweb.com links you to information about periods and types of architecture as well.

APPENDIX

Where to Buy Stuff

Ordering supplies and equipment from mail-order catalogs can help you save time and money.

Batteries

Batteries
2301 Robb Drive
Reno, NV 89523
Telephone number: 800-BATTERIES
Website address: www.1800Batteries.com
Look here for cellular telephone batteries.

Books

AIA Bookstore
1735 New York Avenue, NW
Washington, DC 20006-5292

Telephone number for books: 888-ARCH-115
Telephone number for documents: 800-365-2724
Facsimile number: 802-864-7626
Website address: www.aiabooks.com

Amazon.com

Website address: www.amazon.com

Architects and Designers Book Service

P.O. Box 6002
Delran, NJ 08370

Telephone number: 800-363-4821
Website address: www.booksonline.com

Barnes and Noble

One Pond Road
Rockleigh, NJ 07657

Telephone number: 800-THE-BOOK (800-843-2665)
Facsimile number: 800-767-9169
Website address: www.bn.com or on AOL- Keyword: bn

Edward R. Hamilton, Bookseller

Falls Village, CT 06031-5000

Telephone number: none available
Website address: www.hamiltonbook.com
Look here for drastically reduced prices on all kinds of architecture books.

McGraw-Hill, Inc.

Customer Services
P.O. Box 545
Blacklick, OH 43004-0545

Telephone number: 800-722-4726
Facsimile number: 614-755-5645
Website address: www.books.mcgraw-hill.com

W. W. Norton & Company, Inc.

500 Fifth Avenue
New York, NY 10110

Telephone number: 800-233-4830
Facsimile number: 800-458-6515
Website address: web.wwnorton.com:80/npb.htm

Prairie Avenue Bookshop

711 South Dearborn
Chicago, IL 60605

Telephone number: 800-474-2724
Facsimile number: 312-922-5184

Reid & Wright: An Antiquarian Book Center

287 New Milford Turnpike, Route 202
New Preston, CT 06777

Telephone number: 860-868-7706
Facsimile number: 860-868-1242
Look here for out-of-print architecture books.

John Wiley & Sons, Inc. and Preservation Press

Distribution Center
1 Wiley Drive
Somerset, NJ 08875-1272

Telephone number: 732-469-4400
Facsimile number: 732-302-2300
E-mail address: custserv@wiley.com
Website address: www.wiley.com

Checks

Artistic Checks
P.O. Box 1501
Elmira, NY 14902-1501

Telephone number: 800-CHECKSS
Look here for business and computer checks.

Equipment

QVC
1365 Enterprise Drive
West Chester, PA 19380

Telephone number: 800-345-1515
Website address: www.qvc.com
Look here for telephone equipment, audio-visual equipment, computers.

Hardware

Ace Hardware
Telephone number: 800-441-4223
Look here for all hardware, picture hanging kits, spray paint.

Office furnishings, storage systems, and organizers

Ballard Designs
1670 DeFoor Avenue, NW
Atlanta, GA 30318-7528

Telephone number: 800-367-2775
Facsimile number: 800-989-4510
Look here for storage systems.

Hold Everything
Mail Order Department
P.O. Box 7807
San Francisco, CA 94120-7807

Telephone number: 800-421-2264
Facsimile number: 702-363-2541
Look here for organizers, storage systems.

Pottery Barn
Mail Order Department
P.O. Box 7044
San Francisco, CA 94120-7044

Telephone number: 800-922-5507
Facsimile number: 702-363-2541
Look here for organizers, storage systems, picture frames.

Reliable Home Office
P.O. Box 1501
Ottawa, IL 61350-9916

Telephone number: 800-869-6000
Facsimile number: 800-326-3233
Look here for organizers.

Photo storage and cataloging

Century Photo Products & Accessories
P.O. Box 2393
Brea, CA 92822

Telephone number: 800-767-0777
Facsimile number: 800-786-7939
Website address: www.20thcenturydirect.com
Look here for photograph, slides and negatives sleeves.

Picture frames

Graphik Dimensions, Ltd.
2103 Brentwood Street
High Point, NC 27263

Telephone number: 800-221-0262
Facsimile number: 336-887-3773
Website address: www.graphikdimensions.com

Postage stamps

e-Stamp
Website address: e-stamp.com
E-Stamp Internet Postage is a service approved by the United States Postal Service that allows you to buy and print postage from your personal computer, provided you have a CD-ROM drive, a laser or inkjet printer, and access to the internet. Check the e-Stamp Website for terms.

Stamps.com

Website address: www.stamps.com

Stamps.com is a service regulated by the United States Postal Service that allows you to buy and print postage from your personal computer, provided you have a CD-ROM drive, a laser or inkjet printer, and access to the internet. Check the Stamps.com Website for terms.

Stamp Fulfillment Services

P.O. Box 7247
Philadelphia, PA 19101-9014

Telephone number: 800STAMP24
Facsimile number: 816-545-1212

USA Philatelic

P.O. Box 419424
Kansas City, MO 64141-6424

Supplies, art

Dick Blick Art Materials

P.O. Box 1267
Galesburg, IL 61402-1267

Telephone number: 800-447-8192
Facsimile number: 800-621-8293
e-mail address: info@dickblick.com
Look here for signage materials, colored paper, artists materials, mat boards, colored pencils.

Supplies, drafting

Charrette Corporation
31 Olympia Avenue
Box 4010
Woburn, MA 01888-4010

Telephone number: 800-367-DRAW
Facsimile number: 800-626-7889
E-mail address: custserv@charrette.com
Website address: www.charrette.com
Look here for gadgets, specialty papers, portfolios, presentation materials.

Dataprint Corporation
700 South Claremont Street
P.O. Box 5910
San Mateo, CA 94402

Telephone number: 800-227-6191
Facsimile number: 800-232-1295
Website address: www.dataprint.com
Look here for adhesive-backed film.

Supplies, graphic

GS Direct, Inc.
7480 West 78th Street
Bloomington, MN 55439-2513

Telephone number: 800-234-DRAW
Facsimile number: 612-942-0216
E-mail address: gscatalog@aol.com
Website address: www.artproducts.com/mweb/gsdirect.htm
Look here for white mailing and storage tubes, sales on drafting supplies, portable drafting tables.

Supplies, office and equipment

Viking Office Products
P.O. Box 61144
Los Angeles, CA 90061
P.O. Box 1052
E. Windsor, CT 06088
P.O. Box 465644
Cincinnati, OH 45246
P.O. Box 819064
Dallas, TX 75381

Telephone number: 800-421-1222
Facsimile number: 800-SNAPFAX
Website address: www.vikingop.com
Look here for business stationery, novelty paper, colored envelopes.

Wholesale Supply Company
P.O. Box 23437
Nashville, TN 37202

Telephone number: 800-962-9162
Facsimile number: 800-962-4FAX
Website address: www.wholesalesupply.com
This company sells to businesses only.
Look here for all stationery, office supplies, computer supplies, equipment, furniture.

APPENDIX C

Standardized Forms

The 20 standardized office forms in this section are designed to help you implement some of the tips, tactics and techniques mentioned in *The Architect's Business Problem Solver.* They are organized according to the five sections of this book. They are also available on the disk provided with this book. Experiment with using the forms as they are and then customize them for your practice.

C.1 Business Plan Worksheet Form

Use the form on the next page as a guide to putting together a business plan for your practice.

Business Plan Worksheet

INTRODUCTION

Company name _____

Address _____

Telephone number _____

Facsimile number _____

e-Mail address _____

Contact person _____

Paragraph about company

_____

_____

_____

_____

_____

Design expertise

_____

_____

_____

Target markets

_____

_____

_____

Financial requirements

_____

_____

_____

Business Plan Worksheet (continued)

Term of loan, operating line of credit, mortgage, etc.

_____

Summary of proposed use of funds

_____

_____

_____

_____

_____

FIRM'S CONCEPT

Table of contents (attach)

Summary of firm with highlights

_____

_____

_____

_____

_____

_____

_____

_____

_____

_____

_____

_____

_____

_____

_____

Business Plan Worksheet (continued)

Forecast of the design profession and its growth potential

_____

_____

_____

_____

General markets

_____

_____

_____

The competition

_____

_____

_____

National and economic trends

_____

_____

_____

Business goals: one year, long range

_____

_____

_____

Marketing plan (attach)

Experience

_____

_____

_____

Business Plan Worksheet (continued)

Target markets

_____

_____

_____

Forecasts: one month, first year, long range

_____

_____

_____

FINANCIAL PLAN

Financial forecast

_____

_____

_____

_____

Preliminary balance sheet (attach)

Income and expense forecast statement (attach)

Cash flow forecast (attach)

Financing needs (attach)

Loans (attach)

APPENDIX

List of references: banker, accountant, attorney, insurance agent

_____

_____

_____

Business Plan Worksheet (continued)

Personal net worth statement (attach)

Summary of business insurance coverage

_____

_____

_____

Accounts receivable summary (attach)

Accounts payable summary (attach)

Legal agreements

_____

_____

_____

Financial statements for company (attach)

Copy of company brochure (attach)

News articles on firm (attach)

FIRM'S OPERATION

Location and space _____

_____

 Staffing required

_____

_____

_____

Equipment required

_____

_____

_____

Business Plan Worksheet (continued)

Business structure: Sole proprietorship, Partnership, Corporation

_____

_____

_____

_____

List of officers

_____

_____

_____

_____

List of contracts with clients

_____

_____

_____

_____

Background of key personnel

_____

_____

_____

_____

Organizational chart (attach)

Action plan (attach)

Business Plan Worksheet (continued)

Steps to accomplish this year's goals

_____

_____

_____

_____

_____

Schedule outlining checkpoints throughout year

_____

_____

_____

_____

_____

C.2 Questionnaire for Prospective Clients

Use the form on the next page when you talk to a prospective client for the first time. Using this form helps you to weed out projects in which you have no interest and sets you up for an informed first meeting with a prospective client. Consider printing it on colored paper to distinguish it from other papers in your office.

Questionnaire for Prospective Clients

Date: ___/___/___

Client: _____

Address: _____

_____

Telephone: _____

How did you hear about me?

_____

_____

What is the scope of your project?

_____

_____

What is your budget? Is there a contingency included in that budget?

_____

_____

What is your time schedule?

_____

_____

Have you ever worked with an architect?

_____

_____

How did you come to hire that architect?

_____

_____

Did the architect provide drawings, or a full line of services?

_____

_____

Are you familiar with the phases of a typical project and the services provided during those phases?

_____

Questionnaire for Prospective Clients (continued)

What do you expect to gain by working with an architect?

_____

_____

Have you ever renovated, added on, or built before?

_____

_____

Have you every worked with a general contractor?

_____

_____

How did you come to hire that general contractor?

_____

_____

Do you do any home improvement yourself?

_____

_____

What style of architecture do you prefer?

_____

_____

How aware are you of current design trends, materials, appliances, and fixtures?

_____

_____

Do you have pictures or clippings of the interior design or architecture you prefer?

_____

_____

How would you describe your decision-making process relative to design choices?

_____

_____

C.3 Follow-up Questionnaire for Completed Projects Form

Use the form on the next page to guide a discussion with your clients about the successes and failures of their projects. Although the questionnaire deals with the projects themselves, it is still a good barometer for assessing your ability to build good client-architect relationships. Consider printing it on colored paper to distinguish it from other papers in your office.

Follow-up Questionnaire for Completed Projects

Date _____/_____/_____

Client: _____

Address: _____

Telephone no.: _____

How is the project similar to how you imagined it would be?

_____

_____

How is the project different from how you imagined it would be?

_____

_____

Describe how the phases used by the architect to develop the project helped or hindered the project's design. _____

_____

What do you remember about the design process as being interesting, boring, useful, useless, appropriate, inappropriate? _____

_____

How would you assess the drawings' portrayal of what the project would look like?

_____

_____

What, if anything, would you change about the way the project was developed on paper?

_____

Should there have been more information on the drawings? Less information?

_____

Follow-up Questionnaire for Completed Projects (continued)

What, if anything, were you concerned about when construction began in terms of success-fully executing the design? _____

_____

Did the architect keep you well informed of the options, changes, and other information important to the project? _____

_____

What did you expect to gain by working with an architect? _____

_____

What is the most surprising aspect of the built project? _____

_____

Now that it is complete, assess the time element of the project. How do you recall it? What caused lags in the time frame? What would you say to friends about the time factor?

_____

_____

Do you believe that you could recoup your investment if you put your house on the market today? _____

What are the components or areas that caused the price to go up?

_____

Relative to the cost to build the project, how do you regard the architect's fees?

_____

_____

_____

_____

_____

_____

Follow-up Questionnaire for Completed Projects (continued)

Relative to the architect's billing procedure, were you prepared for the amounts requested each month? Would you have preferred more frequent or less frequent billings? Would you have preferred to pay on an installment plan over the length of the project? Were you reluctant to pay a bill if you had not received updated drawings or specifications or some other physical evidence of the work being done by the architect?

_____

_____

_____

_____

_____

Describe what you would change about the project if you could do it all over again. Is there anything you plan to change in the near future? If so, what?

_____

_____

_____

_____

_____

C.4 Employment Offer Checklist Form

Use the form on the next page to prepare a job offer to a prospective employee.

Employment Offer Checklist

Date: ___/___/___

Candidate: _____

Address: _____

Telephone no.: _____

1. Title of the position _____

2. Duties and responsibilities _____

_____

_____

3. Name and title of person to whom new employee reports _____

_____

4. Office location to which new employee is assigned _____

_____

5. Base salary in terms of amount and frequency of payment _____

6. Overtime requirements and basis for payment _____

7. Terms of benefits package _____

8. Date by which candidate must accept or reject job offer _____

9. Start date _____

10. Number of hours to be worked each week _____

11. Dates of first performance or salary reviews_____

12. Perks _____

_____

_____

13. Specifics of relocation package _____

14. Reasons why the candidate might be able to advance beyond the position being offered

_____

_____

C.5 Job Performance Standards Outline Form

Use the form on the next page to set job performance standards for the various positions in your firm.

Job Performance Standards Outline

The 5 Ws and 1 H of job performance standards

WHO
Who is the employee? _____

WHAT
What are the employee's responsibilities, one by one? _____

_____

_____

_____

_____

WHEN
When will the responsibilities be performed, and in what time frame? _____

_____

_____

WHERE
Where and under what circumstances will the responsibilities be fulfilled? _____

_____

_____

WHY
Why are the responsibilities important as they relate to the advancement of the employee and the vitality of the practice at large?

_____

_____

HOW
How will the employee fulfill these responsibilities? In other words, what is the standard of care? _____

_____

_____

C.6 Telephone Call Log Form

Use the form on the next page to keep track of long distance telephone calls you make so that you can charge them to your clients. Use this form if you do not subscribe to a long-distance telephone service that offers accounting codes. Consider printing it on colored paper to distinguish it from other papers in your office.

Telephone Call Log

Month: _____ Year:_____

Day	Time	Telephone no.	Proj. no.	Party called
____	____:____ AM PM	(___) ___-_____	_____	_____
____	____:____ AM PM	(___) ___-_____	_____	_____
____	____:____ AM PM	(___) ___-_____	_____	_____
____	____:____ AM PM	(___) ___-_____	_____	_____
____	____:____ AM PM	(___) ___-_____	_____	_____
____	____:____ AM PM	(___) ___-_____	_____	_____
____	____:____ AM PM	(___) ___-_____	_____	_____
____	____:____ AM PM	(___) ___-_____	_____	_____
____	____:____ AM PM	(___) ___-_____	_____	_____
____	____:____ AM PM	(___) ___-_____	_____	_____
____	____:____ AM PM	(___) ___-_____	_____	_____
____	____:____ AM PM	(___) ___-_____	_____	_____
____	____:____ AM PM	(___) ___-_____	_____	_____
____	____:____ AM PM	(___) ___-_____	_____	_____
____	____:____ AM PM	(___) ___-_____	_____	_____
____	____:____ AM PM	(___) ___-_____	_____	_____
____	____:____ AM PM	(___) ___-_____	_____	_____
____	____:____ AM PM	(___) ___-_____	_____	_____
____	____:____ AM PM	(___) ___-_____	_____	_____
____	____:____ AM PM	(___) ___-_____	_____	_____
____	____:____ AM PM	(___) ___-_____	_____	_____
____	____:____ AM PM	(___) ___-_____	_____	_____
____	____:____ AM PM	(___) ___-_____	_____	_____
____	____:____ AM PM	(___) ___-_____	_____	_____

C.7 Telephone Conversation Record Form

Use the form on the next page to record notes during telephone conversations. Keep it in a three-ring binder near the telephone or in a project notebook. Consider printing this form on colored paper to distinguish it from other papers in your office, especially those kept in project notebooks.

Telephone Conversation Record

____/____/____ at ____:____ AM PM to ____:____ AM PM   Min ____

Regarding PROJECT NUMBER _____, the following individual contacted me/was contacted by me:

_____

_____

_____

This individual may be contacted at:

TELEPHONE NUMBER   Home (_____) _____ - _____

Work (_____) _____ - _____

Ext. _____

Cell (_____) _____ - _____

Fax (_____) _____ - _____

Page (_____) _____ - _____

The following was discussed:

_____

_____

_____

_____

_____

_____

_____

_____

_____

_____

_____

SIGNED: _____

C.8 Telephone Message Form

Use the sheet on the next page to record telephone messages left on your answering machine or voice mail. Also, use it to keep track of messages you leave. At the end of the month, this form serves as a reminder of what has transpired by way of telephone calls.

Make up a little booklet by printing 10 sheets on both sides, stacking them, folding them in half lengthwise, and stapling them on the fold. Your finished booklet will be $4^{1}/_{4}$ inches wide by 11 inches tall. Make your own cover.

It is worth the time to make up the booklet because it is more useful than the ready-made telephone message booklets that are available at stationery stores.

Date: ___/___/___ Time: _____ AM PM

I called/was called by:

_____

Telephone no.   Home (_____) _____-_____

                Work (_____) _____-_____

                        Ext._____

                Cell (_____) _____-_____

                Fax (_____) _____-_____

                Page (_____) _____-_____

My/Their message:

_____

_____

_____

Return call___/___/___ They'll call back _____

Date: ___/___/___ Time: _____ AM PM

I called/was called by:

_____

Telephone no.   Home (_____) _____-_____

                Work (_____) _____-_____

                        Ext._____

                Cell (_____) _____-_____

                Fax (_____) _____-_____

                Page (_____) _____-_____

My/Their message:

_____

_____

_____

Return call___/___/___ They'll call back _____

Date: ___/___/___ Time: _____ AM PM

I called/was called by:

_____

Telephone no.   Home (_____) _____-_____

                Work (_____) _____-_____

                        Ext._____

                Cell (_____) _____-_____

                Fax (_____) _____-_____

                Page (_____) _____-_____

My/Their message:

_____

_____

_____

Return call___/___/___ They'll call back _____

Date: ___/___/___ Time: _____ AM PM

I called/was called by:

_____

Telephone no.   Home (_____) _____-_____

                Work (_____) _____-_____

                        Ext._____

                Cell (_____) _____-_____

                Fax (_____) _____-_____

                Page (_____) _____-_____

My/Their message:

_____

_____

_____

Return call___/___/___ They'll call back _____

C.9 Master To-Do List Form

This master to-do list form on the next page will help you get started making one of your own. Because a master to-do list is all-inclusive, it probably will exceed two pages. Be creative in the way you put together your master to-do list, since it really is the map to your success. Consider formatting it like a spread sheet, or tape several pages together, accordion style. However you do it, make sure that it is something to which you want to refer regularly.

Master To-Do List

Date _____/_____/_____

Twenty-five potential categories are listed alphabetically:

Architecture projects _____

_____

_____

_____

_____

_____

Automobiles _____

Cleaning _____

Competitions _____

Correspondence _____

_____

_____

Courses _____

_____

_____

Errands _____

_____

_____

Invoices _____

Legal matters _____

Marketing _____

_____

Master To-Do List (continued)

Meetings _____

_____

_____

Money matters _____

_____

_____

Office chores _____

_____

Personal chores _____

_____

_____

Personal development _____

_____

Pet projects _____

_____

_____

Portfolio _____

_____

Professional development _____

_____

_____

Promotion _____

_____

Master To-Do List (continued)

Purchases _____

_____

_____

Reading _____

_____

_____

Research _____

_____

Resume _____

Teaching _____

_____

_____

Telephone calls _____

_____

_____

Travel _____

_____

_____

Visiting _____

_____

_____

Writing _____

_____

C.10 Daily To-Do List Form

Use the form on the next page to list the tasks you want to accomplish each day by culling them from your master to-do list. After you use it for a while, you will be able to modify it to better suit your individual needs.

Daily To-Do List for ____/____/____

TELEPHONE CALLS

Project no.	Party	Regarding
_____	_____	_____
_____	_____	_____
_____	_____	_____
_____	_____	_____
_____	_____	_____
_____	_____	_____
_____	_____	_____
_____	_____	_____

APPOINTMENTS

Project no.	Time	Place
_____	_____	_____
_____	_____	_____
_____	_____	_____
_____	_____	_____
_____	_____	_____
_____	_____	_____
_____	_____	_____

Daily To-Do List (continued)

<u>PROJECTS</u>

Project no.   To do

_____   _____

_____   _____

_____   _____

_____   _____

_____   _____

_____   _____

_____   _____

_____   _____

_____   _____

_____   _____

<u>ERRANDS</u>

Project no.   To do

_____   _____

_____   _____

_____   _____

_____   _____

_____   _____

_____   _____

Daily To-Do List (continued)

PURCHASES AND ORDERS

Project no.   **Purchase or order**

_____   _____

_____   _____

_____   _____

_____   _____

_____   _____

_____   _____

CHORES AND TASKS

Project no.   **Chore or task**

_____   _____

_____   _____

_____   _____

_____   _____

_____   _____

C.11 Meeting Notes Form

Use the form on the next page for taking notes at meetings. Consider printing it on colored paper to distinguish it from other papers in your office, especially those kept in project notebooks.

Meeting Notes ____ / ____ / ____

____:____ AM PM to ____:____ AM PM

Project name _____

Project number _____

Parties present:

_____

_____

_____

_____

The following was observed or discussed:

_____

_____

_____

_____

_____

_____

_____

_____

_____

_____

_____

_____

Signed: _____

(more)

_____

_____

_____

_____

_____

_____

_____

_____

_____

_____

_____

_____

_____

_____

_____

_____

As a result of or to follow up this meeting, I will:

_____

_____

_____

_____

_____

Meeting Notes Form

C.12 Startup Money Checklist Form

Use the form on the next page to determine which of these costs associated with opening a business apply to your new practice.

Startup Money Checklist

Business license   _____

Professional license   _____

Rental deposit on office   _____

Telephone installation and deposits   _____

Utility deposits   _____

Insurance

     Health   _____

     General liability   _____

     Professional liability   _____

     Life   _____

     Theft   _____

     Disability   _____

Legal

     Initial consultation   _____

     Form of business papers   _____

Accounting

     Initial consultation   _____

     Format resolution   _____

Dues for professional organizations

     Local   _____

     State   _____

     National   _____

Startup Money Checklist (continued)

Advertising

      Advertisements _____

      Brochures _____

Stationery

      Business cards _____

      Letterhead _____

      Envelopes _____

      Mailing labels _____

      Other _____

      Other _____

      Other _____

      Other _____

Equipment

      Computer _____

      Computer software _____

      Printer(s) _____

      Scanner _____

      Typewriter _____

      Telephone(s) _____

      Answering machine _____

      Facsimile machine _____

      Calculator _____

      Photocopier _____

Startup Money Checklist Form.

Startup Money Checklist (continued)

    Blueprint machine   _____

    Camera   _____

    Stereo   _____

    Television   _____

    Videocassette recorder   _____

    Other   _____

    Other   _____

    Other   _____

    Other   _____

Supplies

    Pencils, pens   _____

    Toner   _____

    Ink cartridges, ribbons   _____

    Paper(s)   _____

    Drafting implements   _____

    Paper clips   _____

    Rubber bands   _____

    Stapler and staples   _____

    Notebooks   _____

    Other   _____

    Other   _____

    Other   _____

    Other   _____

Startup Money Checklist (continued)

Furniture

       Desk _____

       Drafting table(s) _____

       Computer station _____

       Chair(s) _____

       Lamp(s) _____

       Bookcases _____

       File cabinets _____

       Storage cabinets _____

       Other _____

       Other _____

       Other _____

       Other _____

TOTAL _____

C.13 Financial Needs Checklist Form

Use the form on the next page to determine financial needs to support your personal life.

Financial Needs Checklist

Residence

     Monthly payment   _____

     Taxes   _____

     Insurance   _____

Utilities

     Water   _____

     Telephone   _____

     Heat and air conditioning   _____

     Electricity   _____

Clothing

     Yours   _____

     Spouse's   _____

     Children's   _____

Food   _____

Automobile   _____

     Payment   _____

     Gas   _____

     Maintenance   _____

     Insurance   _____

     Registration   _____

Credit

     Credit cards   _____

Financial Needs Checklist (continued)

     Installment loans   _____

     Student loans   _____

Other

     Life insurance   _____

     Education   _____

     Medical and dental   _____

     Taxes   _____

     Recreation   _____

     Travel   _____

     Donations   _____

     Health insurance   _____

TOTAL   _____

C.14 Billable Hours Tally Sheet Form

You and your employees use the form on the next page to keep track of the hours you spend on any given project as well as the hours you spend on office-related tasks. Forms are provided for the first and second halves of the month.

Record of Billable Hours Worked

Period A for _____, _____

Name: _____

Phase of Project:

0. Prephase   1. Schematic design   2. Design development   3. Construction documents
4. Bidding   5. Construction administration   6. Postphase/add'l services

Project number

Phase	0	1	2	3	4	5	6	0	1	2	3	4	5	6	0	1	2	3	4	5	6
Day 1	_	_	_	_	_	_	_	_	_	_	_	_	_	_	_	_	_	_	_	_	_
2	_	_	_	_	_	_	_	_	_	_	_	_	_	_	_	_	_	_	_	_	_
3	_	_	_	_	_	_	_	_	_	_	_	_	_	_	_	_	_	_	_	_	_
4	_	_	_	_	_	_	_	_	_	_	_	_	_	_	_	_	_	_	_	_	_
5	_	_	_	_	_	_	_	_	_	_	_	_	_	_	_	_	_	_	_	_	_
6	_	_	_	_	_	_	_	_	_	_	_	_	_	_	_	_	_	_	_	_	_
7	_	_	_	_	_	_	_	_	_	_	_	_	_	_	_	_	_	_	_	_	_
8	_	_	_	_	_	_	_	_	_	_	_	_	_	_	_	_	_	_	_	_	_
9	_	_	_	_	_	_	_	_	_	_	_	_	_	_	_	_	_	_	_	_	_
10	_	_	_	_	_	_	_	_	_	_	_	_	_	_	_	_	_	_	_	_	_
11	_	_	_	_	_	_	_	_	_	_	_	_	_	_	_	_	_	_	_	_	_
12	_	_	_	_	_	_	_	_	_	_	_	_	_	_	_	_	_	_	_	_	_
13	_	_	_	_	_	_	_	_	_	_	_	_	_	_	_	_	_	_	_	_	_
14	_	_	_	_	_	_	_	_	_	_	_	_	_	_	_	_	_	_	_	_	_
15	_	_	_	_	_	_	_	_	_	_	_	_	_	_	_	_	_	_	_	_	_
Total	_	_	_	_	_	_	_	_	_	_	_	_	_	_	_	_	_	_	_	_	_

Signed: _____

Record of Nonbillable Hours Worked

Period A for _____, _____

Name: _____

Office

Office activity codes

BK: Bookkeeping	CL: Cleaning	CO:Competition	DE:Decorating
GN: General	IN: Invoicing	LI: Library	MK:Marketing
PA: Payroll	PU:Purchases	SA: Samples	SO: Solicitor
TX: Taxes			

Phase	BK	CL	CO	DE	GN	IN	LI	MK	PA	PU	SA	SO	TX
Day 1	___	___	___	___	___	___	___	___	___	___	___	___	___
2	___	___	___	___	___	___	___	___	___	___	___	___	___
3	___	___	___	___	___	___	___	___	___	___	___	___	___
4	___	___	___	___	___	___	___	___	___	___	___	___	___
5	___	___	___	___	___	___	___	___	___	___	___	___	___
6	___	___	___	___	___	___	___	___	___	___	___	___	___
7	___	___	___	___	___	___	___	___	___	___	___	___	___
8	___	___	___	___	___	___	___	___	___	___	___	___	___
9	___	___	___	___	___	___	___	___	___	___	___	___	___
10	___	___	___	___	___	___	___	___	___	___	___	___	___
11	___	___	___	___	___	___	___	___	___	___	___	___	___
12	___	___	___	___	___	___	___	___	___	___	___	___	___
13	___	___	___	___	___	___	___	___	___	___	___	___	___
14	___	___	___	___	___	___	___	___	___	___	___	___	___
15	___	___	___	___	___	___	___	___	___	___	___	___	___
Total	___	___	___	___	___	___	___	___	___	___	___	___	___

Billable Hours Tally Sheet Form

Record of Billable Hours Worked

Period B for _____, _____

Name: _____

Phase of Project:

0. Prephase   1. Schematic design   2. Design development   3. Construction documents
4. Bidding   5. Construction administration   6. Postphase/add'l services

Project number

Phase	0	1	2	3	4	5	6	0	1	2	3	4	5	6	0	1	2	3	4	5	6
Day 16	__	__	__	__	__	__	__	__	__	__	__	__	__	__	__	__	__	__	__	__	__
17	__	__	__	__	__	__	__	__	__	__	__	__	__	__	__	__	__	__	__	__	__
18	__	__	__	__	__	__	__	__	__	__	__	__	__	__	__	__	__	__	__	__	__
19	__	__	__	__	__	__	__	__	__	__	__	__	__	__	__	__	__	__	__	__	__
20	__	__	__	__	__	__	__	__	__	__	__	__	__	__	__	__	__	__	__	__	__
21	__	__	__	__	__	__	__	__	__	__	__	__	__	__	__	__	__	__	__	__	__
22	__	__	__	__	__	__	__	__	__	__	__	__	__	__	__	__	__	__	__	__	__
23	__	__	__	__	__	__	__	__	__	__	__	__	__	__	__	__	__	__	__	__	__
24	__	__	__	__	__	__	__	__	__	__	__	__	__	__	__	__	__	__	__	__	__
25	__	__	__	__	__	__	__	__	__	__	__	__	__	__	__	__	__	__	__	__	__
26	__	__	__	__	__	__	__	__	__	__	__	__	__	__	__	__	__	__	__	__	__
27	__	__	__	__	__	__	__	__	__	__	__	__	__	__	__	__	__	__	__	__	__
28	__	__	__	__	__	__	__	__	__	__	__	__	__	__	__	__	__	__	__	__	__
29	__	__	__	__	__	__	__	__	__	__	__	__	__	__	__	__	__	__	__	__	__
30	__	__	__	__	__	__	__	__	__	__	__	__	__	__	__	__	__	__	__	__	__
31	__	__	__	__	__	__	__	__	__	__	__	__	__	__	__	__	__	__	__	__	__
Total	__	__	__	__	__	__	__	__	__	__	__	__	__	__	__	__	__	__	__	__	__

Signed: _____

Record of Nonbillable Hours Worked

Period A for _____, _____

Name: _____

Office

Office activity codes

BK: Bookkeeping	CL: Cleaning	CO: Competition	DE: Decorating
GN: General	IN: Invoicing	LI: Library	MK: Marketing
PA: Payroll	PU: Purchases	SA: Samples	SO: Solicitor
TX: Taxes			

Phase	BK	CL	CO	DE	GN	IN	LI	MK	PA	PU	SA	SO	TX
Day 16	___	___	___	___	___	___	___	___	___	___	___	___	___
17	___	___	___	___	___	___	___	___	___	___	___	___	___
18	___	___	___	___	___	___	___	___	___	___	___	___	___
19	___	___	___	___	___	___	___	___	___	___	___	___	___
20	___	___	___	___	___	___	___	___	___	___	___	___	___
21	___	___	___	___	___	___	___	___	___	___	___	___	___
22	___	___	___	___	___	___	___	___	___	___	___	___	___
23	___	___	___	___	___	___	___	___	___	___	___	___	___
24	___	___	___	___	___	___	___	___	___	___	___	___	___
25	___	___	___	___	___	___	___	___	___	___	___	___	___
26	___	___	___	___	___	___	___	___	___	___	___	___	___
27	___	___	___	___	___	___	___	___	___	___	___	___	___
28	___	___	___	___	___	___	___	___	___	___	___	___	___
29	___	___	___	___	___	___	___	___	___	___	___	___	___
30	___	___	___	___	___	___	___	___	___	___	___	___	___
31	___	___	___	___	___	___	___	___	___	___	___	___	___
Total	___	___	___	___	___	___	___	___	___	___	___	___	___

Nonbillable Hours Tally Sheet Form

C.15 Individual Expenses Record Form

Use the form on the next page to keep track of out-of-pocket expenses. Essentially, it is an expense report that you or your employees can use. Consider printing it on colored paper to distinguish it from other papers in your office.

Individual Expenses Record

Date _____/_____/_____

Name: _____

Project number: _____ _____ _____ _____ _____ _____ _____ _____ Office

COMMUNICATIONS

Telephone calls ___ ___ ___ ___ ___ ___ ___ ___

Facsimile ___ ___ ___ ___ ___ ___ ___ ___

DELIVERIES

U.S. mail ___ ___ ___ ___ ___ ___ ___ ___

Carrier ___ ___ ___ ___ ___ ___ ___ ___

Messenger ___ ___ ___ ___ ___ ___ ___ ___

COPYING

Blueprints ___ ___ ___ ___ ___ ___ ___ ___

Photocopies ___ ___ ___ ___ ___ ___ ___ ___

SUPPLIES

Film, processing ___ ___ ___ ___ ___ ___ ___ ___

Office supplies ___ ___ ___ ___ ___ ___ ___ ___

Drafting supplies ___ ___ ___ ___ ___ ___ ___ ___

Stationery ___ ___ ___ ___ ___ ___ ___ ___

TRAVEL

Air fares ___ ___ ___ ___ ___ ___ ___ ___

Bus fares ___ ___ ___ ___ ___ ___ ___ ___

Subway fares ___ ___ ___ ___ ___ ___ ___ ___

Individual Expenses Record (continued)

Taxi fares   ___ ___ ___ ___ ___ ___ ___ ___

Train fares   ___ ___ ___ ___ ___ ___ ___ ___

Mileage $.___/mile   ___ ___ ___ ___ ___ ___ ___ ___

Rental car   ___ ___ ___ ___ ___ ___ ___ ___

Lodging   ___ ___ ___ ___ ___ ___ ___ ___

Meals   ___ ___ ___ ___ ___ ___ ___ ___

<u>OTHER</u>

Other   ___ ___ ___ ___ ___ ___ ___ ___

Other   ___ ___ ___ ___ ___ ___ ___ ___

Other   ___ ___ ___ ___ ___ ___ ___ ___

Other   ___ ___ ___ ___ ___ ___ ___ ___

Other   ___ ___ ___ ___ ___ ___ ___ ___

Total columns   ___ ___ ___ ___ ___ ___ ___ ___

Grand total _____   Signed: _____

C.16 Automobile Mileage Record Form

Use the form on the next page to record miles traveled in your automobile as well as tolls and parking fees incurred for specific projects. Make several copies of this form on $8^{1}/_{2} \times 11$ inch paper, both sides. Cut the sheets in half crosswise. Stack the sheets. Fold them in half lengthwise, and staple them in the middle to create a little booklet, $4^{1}/_{4}$ inches wide by $5^{1}/_{2}$ inches high. Make up a cover for it. Keep it in your car.

Date _____ Date _____

Destination _____ Destination _____

Project no. _____ Project no. _____

Mileage _____ Mileage _____

Tolls _____ Tolls _____

Parking fees _____ Parking fees _____

Date _____ Date _____

Destination _____ Destination _____

Project no. _____ Project no. _____

Mileage _____ Mileage _____

Tolls _____ Tolls _____

Parking fees _____ Parking fees _____

Date _____ Date _____

Destination _____ Destination _____

Project no. _____ Project no. _____

Mileage _____ Mileage _____

Tolls _____ Tolls _____

Parking fees _____ Parking fees _____

Date _____ Date _____

Destination _____ Destination _____

Project no. _____ Project no. _____

Mileage _____ Mileage _____

Tolls _____ Tolls _____

Parking fees _____ Parking fees _____

C.17 Fees and Reimbursables Tally Sheet Form

Use the form on the next page to keep track of the hours you or your employees work on a particular project as well as reimbursable expenses. Tally the numbers at the end of the month when you prepare your statements of services. Consider printing this form on colored paper to distinguish it from other papers in your office.

Tally Sheet for Services Rendered and Reimbursable Expenses

Page _____ of _____

Statement of Services Rendered and Reimbursable Expenses Incurred for

the _____ Project, No. _____ for ____/____/____ through____/____/____

SERVICES RENDERED

Phase of Project:

☐ Schematic design ☐ Design development ☐ Construction documents

☐ Bidding ☐ Construction administration ☐ Additional services

Date	Explanation	%/Hours
_____	_____	_____
_____	_____	_____
_____	_____	_____
_____	_____	_____
_____	_____	_____
_____	_____	_____
_____	_____	_____
_____	_____	_____
_____	_____	_____
_____	_____	_____
_____	_____	_____
_____	_____	_____
_____	_____	_____
_____	_____	_____
_____	_____	_____
_____	_____	_____

REIMBURSABLES

Date

_____	**Long-distance telephone**	$_____
_____	**Long-distance telephone**	$_____
_____	**Long-distance telephone**	$_____
_____	**Long-distance telephone**	$_____
_____	**Long-distance telephone**	$_____
_____	**Postage** _____	$_____
_____	**Postage** _____	$_____
_____	**Postage** _____	$_____
_____	**Postage** _____	$_____
_____	**Postage** _____	$_____
_____	**Postage** _____	$_____
_____	**Postage** _____	$_____
_____	**Photocopies** _____	$_____
_____	**Photocopies** _____	$_____
_____	**Photocopies** _____	$_____
_____	**Photocopies** _____	$_____
_____	**Photocopies** _____	$_____
_____	**Blueprints** _____	$_____
_____	**Blueprints** _____	$_____
_____	**Blueprints** _____	$_____
_____	**Blueprints** _____	$_____
_____	**Blueprints** _____	$_____
_____	**Blueprints** _____	$_____
_____	**Miscellaneous** _____	$_____
_____	**Miscellaneous** _____	$_____
_____	**Miscellaneous** _____	$_____
_____	**Miscellaneous** _____	$_____

C.18 Stationery and Drafting Supplies Order Record Form

Use the form on the next page to write down your mail-order catalog order before placing your telephone call. Keep it in a three-ring binder along with the packing slip that comes with your order. It helps you to look up item numbers for products you have ordered before. Consider printing this form on colored paper to distinguish it from other papers in your office.

Stationery and Drafting Supplies Order Record

Date _____/_____/_____

Supplier: _____

Account number: _____

Salesperson: _____

Address: _____

_____

_____

Telephone: _____

Item Number	Quan.	Description (color, size)	Price
_____	_____	_____	_____
_____	_____	_____	_____
_____	_____	_____	_____
_____	_____	_____	_____
_____	_____	_____	_____
_____	_____	_____	_____
_____	_____	_____	_____
_____	_____	_____	_____
_____	_____	_____	_____
_____	_____	_____	_____
_____	_____	_____	_____
_____	_____	_____	_____

Method of payment: _____

Order number: _____

Should arrive in: _____ days

Subtotal: _____

Tax: _____

Insurance: _____

Shipping/handling: _____

TOTAL: _____

Signed: _____

C.19 Outgoing Mail Log Form

Use the form on the next page to record mail sent from your office. It helps you to keep track of when mail is sent out as well as postage expenses throughout the year. Keep your mail log near your stamps and outgoing mailbox. Consider printing this form on colored paper to distinguish it from other papers in your office.

Outgoing Mail Log

Month: _____ Year: _____

Day	Project No.	Addressee/Contents	Postage
____	_____	_____	_____
____	_____	_____	_____
____	_____	_____	_____
____	_____	_____	_____
____	_____	_____	_____
____	_____	_____	_____
____	_____	_____	_____
____	_____	_____	_____
____	_____	_____	_____
____	_____	_____	_____
____	_____	_____	_____
____	_____	_____	_____
____	_____	_____	_____
____	_____	_____	_____
____	_____	_____	_____
____	_____	_____	_____
____	_____	_____	_____
____	_____	_____	_____
____	_____	_____	_____
____	_____	_____	_____
____	_____	_____	_____
____	_____	_____	_____
____	_____	_____	_____
____	_____	_____	_____

Total: _____

C.20 Field Report Form

Use the form on the next page to take notes in the field. Consider printing it on colored paper to distinguish it from other papers in your office.

Field Report ____ / ____ / ____

____:____ AM PM to ____:____ AM PM

Project name _____

Project number _____

Parties present:

_____

_____

_____

_____

The following was observed or discussed:

_____

_____

_____

_____

_____

_____

_____

_____

_____

_____

_____

_____

As a result of or to follow up this field report, I will:

_____

_____

_____

Signed:

APPENDIX

Key Words, Phrases, and Concepts

Refer to the following keys words, phrases, and concepts as you would to a standard glossary.

Seemingly common words listed here may have meanings that are specific to the solutions offered in the preceding pages. See if you can recall the significance of these bywords as they relate to the tips, tactics, and techniques outlined for running your practice.

Or start here to determine with which key words, phrases, and concepts you are already familiar and, more important, with which ones you aren't.

A

accommodate

To **accommodate** is to be considerate of your clients' needs, their schedules, their budgets, and their special interests as they relate to their projects. It is one of the tactics described to win over clients in the eight -**ates** to conciliate.

See 2.22 Retaining Clients

accounting methods: cash or accrual

The **cash method** of accounting records cash when it is received and expenses when they are paid. The **accrual method,** unlike the cash system, which shows only what you have received and not what you have earned, shows income and expenses, whether paid or not.

See 4.25 Choosing an Accounting Method

action plan

An **action plan** is a *road map* for your practice that sets forth the ways in which you will achieve the goals you set for it.

See 1.4   Designing a Road Map
See 1.5   Outlining a Business Plan

ad campaign

An **ad campaign** is a series of advertisements placed to attract potential clients. It is a concentrated effort to run advertisements concurrently in several forms of media and/or to run advertisements consecutively in a particular form of media. An ad campaign demonstrates logic, from the design of the advertisements to the choice of the form of media in which to run them.

See 2.9   Where to Advertise

administrator

Administrator is one of four roles you play as the manager of your architectural firm. As an administrator, you ensure that goals are met for both the architectural projects and the business aspects of your practice.

See 2.5   Playing Manager

advertising budget

With an **advertising budget**, you plan for the amount of money you will spend on all aspects of advertising, from the design of advertisements to the costs associated with running them in publications.

See 2.8   Deciding Whether to Advertise

after-action report

An **after-action report** records what happened during a significant occurrence that is likely to recur.

See 3.1 Avoiding Repeated Mistakes

anticipate

To **anticipate** is to be aware of questions and concerns that may arise among your clients concerning any aspect of the process of designing and building architecture. It is one of the tactics described to win over clients in the eight -**ates** to conciliate.

See 2.22 Retaining Clients

architect practitioner

An **architect practitioner** owns or works in a privately owned architectural firm, not in a corporation or for a government agency, etc.

attachment

Attachment refers to one of two manifestations of resistance in clients whereby clients are involved in their projects to such a great extent that it impedes your progress on their behalf. Attachment's counterpart is **detachment**.

See 2.26 Dealing with Resistance in Clients

automobile mileage record form

An **automobile mileage record form** is a standardized office form for recording expenses incurred while using your car for business.

See 5.13 Stocking stationery
See 5.14 Using Standardized Forms
See C.16 Automobile Mileage Record Form

available

Available is one of the attributes of the right accounting firm for your practice.

See 2.45 Hiring an Accountant

B

billable hours tally sheet form

A **billable hours tally sheet form** is a standardized office form for keeping track of the hours you spend working on any given project.

See 5.13 Stocking Stationery
See 5.14 Using Standardized Forms
See C.14 Billable Hours Tally Sheet Form

bringing order to your practice

Bringing order to your practice is the fundamental reason behind *The Architect's Business Problem Solver*. An organized practice allows you the time to attend to your architecture projects.

See 3.13 Bringing Order to Your Practice

building blocks

The term **building blocks**, as used to name Section 1, characterizes fundamental concepts to understand, essential plans to make, and first steps to take in running an architectural practice. These are *practice principles*.

See Section 1: Building Blocks

business plan

A **business plan** is an agenda by which you run the business side of your practice. It lists the who, what, when, where, why, and how of your business.

See 1.5 Outlining a Business Plan

business plan checklist

A **business plan checklist** is a tool that aids you in preparing a *business plan*.

See 1.5 Outlining a Business Plan

business plan worksheet form

Used to compose a business plan, **a business plan worksheet form** is a standardized office form based on the business plan checklist.

See 1.5 Outlining a Business Plan
See 5.13 Stocking Stationery
See 5.14 Using Standardized Forms
See C.1 Business Plan Worksheet Form

business-size envelope

A **business-size envelope** is also known as a **No. 10 envelope**. It is the envelope commonly used for business correspondence. See *Size A envelope.*

See 5.13 Stocking Stationery

business telephone line

A **business telephone line** refers to business service provided by your local telephone company. With different terms and features from residential or *private line service*, business service usually entitles you to a listing of your firm in the Yellow Pages of your local telephone book.

See 4.13 Opting for a Business Telephone Line

C

calendar year

For tax purposes, a **calendar year** is a 12-month period ending the last day of December. See **fiscal year**.

See 4.23 Reporting and Paying Taxes

Caller ID

Caller ID is a feature offered by some local telephone companies that allows you to see who is calling you on a display screen on a special, but relatively inexpensive, piece of equipment.

See 3.2 Handling Telephone Calls

cash flow

Cash flow refers to the amount and time of cash inflow, for example, incoming fees, in relationship to the amount and time of outflow, such as overhead expenses. It reflects your ability to pay bills when they are due. Adequate cash flow means that enough money is coming in to pay bills when they are due. Cash-flow problems arise when money owed to you does not arrive in time to cover costs. Cash-flow can be looked at daily, monthly, or yearly. It is possible to have adequate yearly cash flow while experiencing monthly cash-flow problems.

See 1.5   Outlining a Business Plan

cash-flow projection

Cash-flow projection charts anticipated fees and other income against anticipated expenditures for your business over a fixed period of time. Used as a supporting document with a business loan application, cash-flow projection is evidence of the viability of your business.

See 4.6   Getting a Business Loan

cash method of accounting

The **cash method of accounting** records cash when it is received and expenses when they are paid as opposed to the accrual method of accounting, which shows income and expenses, whether paid or not.

See 4.25 Choosing an Accounting Method

coercive power

Coercive power is engendered by your employees' fear that you may demote or fire them. Coercive power is one of the three sources of *position power*, which is one of the two forms of a principal's power, along with *personal power*.

See 2.3   Using Your Power to Influence

communicator

Communicator is one of the characteristics of the right accountant for your firm.

See 2.45 Hiring an Accountant

corporation

Here, a **corporation** is an architectural practice that exists as a separate entity from you or you and your partners. Theoretically, its advantage is that you are not personally liable for the corporation's debts, yet in reality, lenders may require you to personally sign for credit or loans. Also, as an architect, you are personally liable for wrongful or negligent acts.

See 1.5   Outlining a Business Plan

D

daily to-do list

A **daily to-do list** is culled from your *master to-do list*. Organized into categories, it states what you want to accomplish in a particular day.

See 3.7   Making a Daily To-Do List

daily to-do list form

A **daily to-do list form** is a *standardized form* that you can use to plan your day.

See 3.5   Keeping a Master To-Do List
See 3.7   Making a Daily To-Do List
See 5.13 Stocking Stationery
See 5.14 Using Standardized Forms
See C.10 Daily To-Do List Form

design

Design is what you define it to be. In the context of this book, design is a byword that is significant in two solutions. First, design is one of the eight reasons to take on a project: The project allows you to display your design talents. Second, design is one of the three aspects of client objections when clients mistakenly believe that you are doing more or doing less than they want.

See 2.14 Deciding to Take on a Project
See 2.19 Fielding Client Objections

design counseling

Design counseling is synonymous with consulting on an hourly basis. Aimed at allowing prospective clients of architectural services the chance to sample working with you before making a commitment to a project, it allows you to exchange ideas during the seminal stage of a project. Unlike other types of consulting, you are compensated on the spot for design counseling services.

See 2.6 Defining a Press Release
See 4.8 Offering Design Counseling Services

detachment

Detachment refers to one of two manifestations of resistance in clients whereby clients do not participate wholly in a project, thereby impeding your progress on their behalf. Detachment's counterpart is **attachment.**

See 2.26 Dealing with Resistance in Clients

direct marketing

Direct marketing refers to contacting prospective clients by telephoning them or by mailing or delivering information about your firm to their doorsteps. It differs from marketing, which is focused on getting prospective clients to contact you after seeing an advertisement or hearing positive publicity about your firm.

See 1.8 Developing a Marketing Plan

disseminator

Disseminator is one of 11 roles in four categories that you play as the principal of your own firm. As a disseminator, you distribute information to your staff that you collect in your role as *monitor* and believe to be useful in your role as *leader*.

See 2.4 Playing Principal

disturbance handler

Disturbance handler is one of 11 roles in four categories that you play as the principal of your own firm. As a disturbance handler, you take care of unexpected interruptions in all areas of your practice.

See 2.4 Playing Principal

E

educate

To **educate** is to be open to opportunities to instruct your clients in the process of designing and building architecture. It is one of the tactics described to win over clients in the eight **-ates** to conciliate.

See 2.22 Retaining Clients

employment offer

An **employment offer** consists of up to 14 points to make about a position you are offering a job candidate. Stated verbally at the time of the offer, it should be extended in writing as a follow-up.

See 2.35 Making an Employment Offer

employment offer checklist form

An **employment offer checklist** *form* is a *standardized form* that helps you prepare a job offer to a prospective employee.

See 2.35 Making an Employment Offer
See 5.13 Stocking Stationery
See 5.14 Using Standardized Forms
See C.4 Employment Offer Checklist Form

entrepreneur

Entrepreneur has two meanings in *The Architect's Business Problem Solver*. First, entrepreneur is one of 11 roles in four categories that you play as the principal of your own firm. As an entrepreneur, you seek new courses along which to move and expand your practice. Second, entrepreneur is one of four roles you play as the manager of your architecture firm. As an entrepreneur, you look for new opportunities for your practice.

See 2.4 Playing Principal
See 2.5 Playing Manager

equity loan

Lending institutions give an **equity loan** against a portion of the actual value of your ownership in real property, such as your house. For example, in the case of your house, the amount of an equity loan would be based on its current market value minus the remaining principal on its mortgage.

See 4.4 Startup Money

estimated income tax

Estimated income tax is paid quarterly by a *sole proprietor* or partners in anticipation of the tax that is figured on *Form 1040* Individual Tax Return for that year. It is equivalent to the tax that was withheld from your paycheck when you were an employee at a firm.

See 4.22 Reviewing Types of Taxes

expectations

In *The Architect's Business Problem Solver*, **expectations** refers to the fourth heading of the mnemonic device devised to help you select the right clients for your practice: PETER points for picking clients.

See 2.13 Picking Clients

experience

Aside from the obvious, **experience** is the second heading of the mnemonic device devised to help you select the right clients for your practice: PETER points for picking clients.

See 2.13 Picking Clients

expert

Expert is one of 11 roles in four categories that you play as the principal of your own firm. As an expert, you develop expertise in all aspects of your practice.

See 2.4 Playing Principal

expert power

Expert power results from the number of your skills, the vastness of your knowledge, or the degree of your expertise. Expert power is one of the three sources of *personal power*, which is one of the two forms of a principal's power, along with *position power*.

See 2.03 Using Your Power to Influence

F

federal and state income taxes

See *income tax.*
See 4.22 Reviewing Types of Taxes

federal unemployment taxes (FUTA)

See *FUTA.* See also *unemployment tax.*
See 4.22 Reviewing Types of Taxes

fees and reimbursables tally sheet form

A **fees and reimbursables tally sheet form** is a standardized form used to keep track of hours you or your employees work on a particular project as well as reimbursable expenses.

See C.17 Fees and Reimbursables Tally Sheet Form

FICA

FICA refers to the Federal Insurance Contributions Act tax, which includes Social Security tax and Medicare tax. See Social Security Taxes.

See 4.22 Reviewing Types of Taxes

field report form

A **field report form** is a standardized form for recording the conditions during a site visit.

See 5.13 Stocking Stationery
See 5.14 Using Standardized Forms
See C.20 Field Report Form

figurehead

Figurehead is one of 11 roles in four categories that you play as the principal of your own firm. As a figurehead, you present your practice in highly visible and symbolically important activities.

See 2.4   Playing Principal

financial needs checklist

A **financial needs checklist** is a tool for determining the financial needs to support your personal life.

See 4.3   Determining Financial Needs
See 5.13 Stocking Stationery
See 5.14 Using Standardized Forms
See C.13 Financial Needs Checklist Form

financial statement

A **financial statement** is one of the tools you use to get a business loan. It lists personal assets beyond the net worth of your house and business.

See 4.6   Getting a Business Loan

fiscal year

For tax purposes, a **fiscal year** is a 12 month period ending the last day of any month but December. A fiscal year that ends on December is known as a calendar year for obvious reasons.

See 4.23 Reporting and Paying Taxes

follow-up questionnaire for completed projects
A **follow-up questionnaire for completed projects** is a *standardized form* that you can use to guide a discussion with your clients about the successes and failures of their projects.

See 5.14 Using Standardized Forms
See C.3 Follow-up Questionnaire For Completed Projects Form

Form 1040
Form 1040 is your Individual Tax Return.

See 4.23 Reporting and Paying Taxes

Form 1065
Form 1065 is used to report net earnings from a *partnership* subject to self-employment tax.

See 4.23 Reporting and Paying Taxes

Form 1120
A corporation files **Form 1120** to pay taxes.

See 4.23 Reporting and Paying Taxes

Form 501
Using **Form 501**, you make payments to the IRS for *income tax* withheld from employees' paychecks.

See 4.22 Reviewing Types of Taxes

French-fold
French-fold is a technique of folding an $8^{1}/_{2} \times 11$ sheet of paper in three sections to fit a *business-size envelope*. A paper that has been French-folded resembles an accordion or folding screen. With a French-fold, letterhead faces outward and toward the

back of an envelope so that the recipient sees who the correspondence is from immediately on opening it.

See 2.7   Writing a Press Release

FUTA
FUTA is the abbreviation for Federal Unemployment Tax. See *unemployment tax.*

See 4.22 Reviewing Types of Taxes

G

geographic locus, geographic scope
Geographic locus or **scope** refers to the location of your practice and the vicinity in which your practice has a presence. Your geographic location comes into play when you are advertising for clients as well as for employees. Depending on the *image* and focus of your practice, your geographical locus or scope can be the city in which you practice, a metropolitan area, or an entire region of the country.

See 2.9   Where to Advertise
See 2.32 Finding New Employees

grounds for firing an employee
Simply stated, the **grounds for firing an employee** are that he or she does not meet the *job performance standards* you set for his or her position.

See 2.37 Setting Job Performance Standards
See 2.40 Dealing with a Marginal Employee
See 2.43 Firing an Employee

H

heart
In *The Architect's Business Problem Solver,* **heart** is one of three human entities of your practice. The heart of your practice is

defined by the desires that drive it. The other entities are *mind* and *soul.*

See 1.1   Running Your Firm

I

image

Image is the personality of your firm. It comes from your *uniqueness* and individuality.

See 1.11 Creating an Image for Your Firm

income tax

Income tax is the payment you make to state and federal governments based on your personal financial gain in a given year. It is separate from *self-employment tax.*

See 4.22 Reviewing Types of Taxes

individual expenses record form

An **individual expenses record form** is a *standardized form* for keeping track of out-of-pocket expenses.

See 5.13 Stocking Stationery
See 5.14 Using Standardized Forms
See C.15 Individual Expenses Record Form

information power

Information power comes from other people's perception that you are privy to information that is not available to them. Information power is one of the three sources of *personal power,* which is one of the two forms of a principal's power, along with *position power.*

See 2.3   Using Your Power to Influence

informed

Informed is one of the attributes of the right accounting firm for your practice.

See 2.45 Hiring an Accountant

initial payment

An **initial payment** is synonymous with a retainer. It is the payment made to bind your agreement with a client. An initial payment is applied against fees for services rendered either in increments during the course of the project or at the end of the project.

See 4.9   Getting Clients to Pay

integrator

Integrator is one of four roles you play as the manager of your architecture firm. As an integrator, you link your other three roles as manager—*producer, administrator,* and *entrepreneur*—with special emphasis on relating to the people involved in the making of architecture.

See 2.5   Playing Manager

J

job description

Part of an *organizational chart,* a **job description** puts in writing the duties to be performed by each of your staff members.

See 1.7   Organizing Your Firm

job performance standards

Job performance standards articulate your expectations of employees by defining the parameters in which they can excel. Typical job performance standards list the who, what, when, where, why, and how of any and every position in your firm. Such standards are essentially your *terms of employment.*

See 2.37 Setting Job Performance Standards
See 2.40 Dealing with a Marginal Employee
See 2.43 Firing an Employee

job performance standards outline form

A **job performance standards outline form** is a *standardized form* that helps you to set *job performance standards* for the various positions in your firm.

job requirements

Job requirements are the skills, training, background, experience, etc. that you articulate when you set about looking for a new employee.

L

leader

Leader is one of 11 roles in four categories that you play as the principal of your own firm. As a leader, you accept responsibility for all the work of your firm.

learning

In this context, **learning** refers to one of the eight reasons to take on a project: The project provides you with an opportunity to learn something important by participating in it.

legitimate power

Legitimate power is the authority you derive from your role as principal of your architectural firm. Legitimate power is one of the three sources of *position power*, which is one of the two forms of a principal's power, along with *personal power*.

letter of introduction

One component in the underlying etiquette prescribed in this book, a **letter of introduction** sent to prospective clients explains your method of working and the fees associated with it.

letter of transmittal

A **letter of transmittal,** also known as a **transmittal,** is a written document that announces and accompanies materials such as drawings, specifications, legal documents, product samples, etc. that are being mailed or delivered. A transmittal can be either in the form of a letter that you compose to serve the particular purpose or in the form of a *standardized form* with blanks that you fill in either by hand or on your computer.

See 2.2   Overcoming Writer's Block

liaison

Liaison is one of 11 roles in four categories that you play as the principal of your own firm. As a liaison, you communicate the goals of your practice to the outside world.

See 2.4   Playing Principal

local

Local is one of the attributes of the right accounting firm for your practice.

See 2.45 Hiring an Accountant

logo

A **logo** is a sign or symbol you use to represent your business. Designing a logo is the third step in defining your firm's *image* as described in this book. The first step is writing a *thesis sentence.* The second step is writing a *slogan.*

See 1.11 Creating an Image for Your Firm

M

marginal employee

A **marginal employee** is one who is failing to meet the *job performance standards* that you set for your firm.

See 2.37 Setting Job Performance Standards

See 2.40 Dealing with a Marginal Employee
See 2.43 Firing an Employee

master to-do list

A **master to-do list** is a menu from which you pick and choose what to do each day. It includes every practical thing and every enjoyable thing you want to do, organized into categories.

See 3.5   Keeping a Master To-Do List

master to-do list form

A **master to-do list form** is a *standardized form* that helps you to compose a *master to-do list.*

See 3.5   Keeping a Master To-Do List
See 5.13 Stocking Stationery
See 5.14 Using Standardized Forms
See C.9   Master To-Do List Form

mediate

To **mediate** is to be available to represent your clients in disputes with participants involved in any of the many aspects of designing and building their projects. It is one of the tactics described to win over clients in the eight **-ates,** to conciliate.

See 2.22 Retaining Clients

meeting notes form

A **meeting notes form** is a *standardized form* on which to jot meeting notes. Better than lined paper, it prompts you for critical information about the time and date of the meeting, parties present, etc.

See 5.13 Stocking Stationery
See 5.14 Using Standardized Forms
See C.11 Meeting Notes Form

message unit

A **message unit** is a predetermined increment of time charged to your monthly telephone bill for telephone calls that you

make. If your telephone account is charged in 5-minute increments, any portion of that 5-minute increment that is used
during a call is charged at the full 5-minute increment. Thus, a
2-minute call will cost the same as a full 5-minute call.

See 4.13 Opting for a Business Telephone Line
See 4.16 Paying for Voice Mail

mind

In *The Architect's Business Problem Solver*, **mind** is one of three
human entities of your practice. Mind relates to the practical
goals that you set with logic. The other entities are *heart* and
soul.

See 1.01 Running Your Firm

mission statement

Defined in architectural terms, a **mission statement** describes
the scale and scope of your practice. A mission statement outlines your unique purpose in running an architecture firm.

See 1.2 Writing a Mission Statement
See 2.21 Allying Your Clients

money

Besides being the topic of Section 4 of this book, **money** is a
byword in two solutions. First, money is one of the eight reasons
to take on a project: The project pays well. Second, money is one
of the three aspects of client objections when clients complain
about your fees.

See 2.14 Deciding to Take on a Project
See 2.19 Fielding Client Objections
See Section 4: Money

monitor

Monitor is one of 11 roles in four categories that you play as the
principal of your own firm. As a monitor, you collect informa-

tion from within and without your firm to keep up with emerging trends.

See 2.04 Playing Principal

N

needs
Needs is one is the components of the *QPN model*. Your clients' needs are typical of those of your market niche.

See 2.21 Allying Your Clients

negotiating
Negotiating is the give-and-take demonstrated between you and your prospective clients in discussing the terms of your agreement with them.

See 2.17 Getting to an Agreement

negotiator
Negotiator is one of 11 roles in four categories that you play as the principal of your own firm. As a negotiator, you work out contracts with clients, consultants, etc. and determine salaries, benefits, etc. for your staff.

See 2.4   Playing Principal

networking
Networking means engaging people in you life's work so that you positively affect their lives and they yours.

See 2.12 Networking

no. 10 envelope
A **no. 10 envelope** is also known as a business-size envelope. It is the envelope commonly used for business correspondence. See Size A envelope.

See 5.13 Stocking Stationery

O

office administrator

An **office administrator** is the individual in your firm who handles the business side of running an architectural practice.

See 2.32 Finding New Employees

office form

See **standardized form**.

See 5.13 Stocking Stationery
See 5.14 Using Standardized Forms
See Appendix C Standardized Forms

open accounts

Open accounts established with local or mail order businesses relieve you of paying on the spot with cash, a check, or a credit card for items purchased or services rendered. Instead, you are billed by the companies, giving you time to arrange funds to cover the costs incurred.

See 4.12 Establishing Open Accounts

organizational chart

Like a bubble diagram that shows the relationships among the program spaces for a building project, an **organizational chart** illustrates the hierarchy of your firm in terms of the people who comprise it.

See 1.5 Outlining a Business Plan
See 1.6 Strategizing for Success
See 1.7 Organizing Your Firm

outgoing mail log form

An **outgoing mail log form** is a *standardized form* used to keep track of the date of and postage for mail that you send out. It is a way of tracking expenses for your projects and a way of keeping track of when mail was sent.

See C.19 Outgoing Mail Log Form

overhead

Overhead is the money required to pay expenses associated with your business. These include fixed costs such as rent and insurance and variable costs such as utility bills and office supplies.

See 4.2   Getting Your Nest Egg Together

P

participate

To **participate** is to be an active participant in all the various teams that work to design and build your clients' projects. It is one of the tactics described to win over clients in the eight -ates to conciliate.

See 2.22 Retaining Clients

partnership

Here, a **partnership** refers to an architectural practice operated by you and a partner or partners. You are responsible for every positive and negative occurrence related to your practice, including those brought about by your partner(s). Although most states do not require formal documentation to establish a partnership, consider drafting a formal partnership agreement that establishes each partner's role.

See 1.05 Outlining a Business Plan
See 4.23 Reporting and Paying Taxes

payroll taxes

Payroll taxes are paid on employees' salaries.

See 4.22 Reviewing Types of Taxes

personal power

Personal power is one of the two forms of a principal's power. It comes from three sources: *referent power*, *information power*, and *expert power*.

See 2.3   Using Your Power to Influence

personality
In *The Architect's Business Problem Solver*, **personality** has two meanings. First, personality is synonymous with the *image* of your firm. Second, personality is the first heading of the mnemonic device devised to help you select the right clients for your practice: PETER points for picking clients.

See 1.11 Creating an Image for Your Firm
See 2.13 Picking Clients

position power
Position power is one of the two forms of a principal's power. It comes from three sources: *legitimate power*, *reward power*, and *coercive power*.

See 2.3 Using Your Power to Influence

power
Power is the personal force you exert to influence others.

See 2.3 Using Your Power to Influence

practice principles
Practice principles are the basic tenets of running your architectural practice. In *The Architect's Business Problem Solver*, they are referred to as **building blocks**.

See Section 1: Building Blocks

practice values
Practice values are the morals and mores that guide you in the running of your practice. They come from the *soul* of your practice.

See 1.1 Running Your Firm
See 1.3 Articulating Your Practice Values

press release
A **press release** is a factual statement that you release to a publication to announce an event or occurrence of interest to its readership.

See 2.6 Defining a Press Release

principal

Principal is one of the characteristics of the right accountant for your firm.

See 2.45 Hiring an Accountant

private-line service

Private-line service refers to residential telephone service that has different terms and features from the business service that supplies your *business telephone line.*

See 4.13 Opting for a Business Telephone Line

problem

For the purposes of this book, a **problem** is defined as any task, any chore, any responsibility, or any concern that takes you away from your drafting board. In addition, a **problem** is defined as a situation that you simply have never encountered before.

problem solver

Besides being the purpose of this book, **problem solver** is one of characteristics of the right accountant for your firm.

See 2.45 Hiring an Accountant

producer

Producer is one of four roles you play as the manager of your architectural firm. As a producer, you actively participate in the architectural projects of your office.

See 2.5 Playing Manager

progress chart

A **progress chart** records the progress of a *marginal employee* so that it can be used as an instrument of discussion and a tool of instruction.

See 2.40 Dealing with a Marginal Employee

progress report

A **progress report** is a telephone call or memorandum that apprises your clients of your progress on their projects.

See 2.27 Maintaining Momentum

project notebook

A **project notebook** is a three ring binder or some such organizer in which all pertinent information having to do with a particular project is kept. To begin with, it might hold important correspondence and completed *telephone conversation record forms* as an account of the project's progress.

See 5.8   Using a Project Notebook

project number

A **project number** gives numerical identification to a project that can be used to organize files and to account for long-distance telephone calls.

See 4.14 Signing Up for Telephone Accounting Codes
See 5.10 Using Project Numbers

prospective client interview notes form

A **prospective client interview notes form** is a *standardized form* that helps you through the initial telephone conversation with a prospective client by prompting you for pertinent information.

See 5.13 Stocking Stationery
See 5.14 Using Standardized Forms
See C.2   Prospective Client Interview Notes Form

public relations

In *The Architect's Business Problem Solver,* **public relations** refers to the steps you take to reach out to and connect with prospective clients as well as the community at large. It refers to your efforts to draw attention to your practice and to establish and protect its image in the public eye.

See 2.8 Deciding Whether to Advertise

purpose

Purpose is one of the components of the *QPN model*. Your purpose is outlined in your *mission statement*. Where it meshes with your client's purpose is your common purpose.

See 1.2   Writing a Mission Statement
See 2.21 Allying Your Clients

Q

QPN model

The **QPN model** is a marketing tool that helps you create a successful alliance between you and your clients when your *qualities* fulfill a common *purpose* that is inspired by their *needs*.

See 2.21 Allying Your Clients

qualitative method to justify a new employee

The Architects' Business Problem Solver discusses two methods for **justifying a new employee,** the **qualitative method** and the **quantitative method.** The qualitative method is based on asking yourself: What could I be doing with the time I spend on tasks that I could delegate to an employee?

See 2.31 Justifying a New Employee
See 4.10 Affording a New Employee

qualities

Qualities is one of the components of the QPN model. Your qualities make you unique. Your *uniqueness* contributes to the *image* of your firm.

See 2.21 Allying Your Clients

quantitative method to justify a new employee

The *Architects' Business Problem Solver* discusses two methods for justifying a new employee, the **quantitative method** and the **qualitative method.** The quantitative method helps you to determine the amount of money you could pay a new employee based on the amount of money it costs for you to handle certain tasks.

See 2.31 Justifying a New Employee
See 4.10 Affording a New Employee

quarterly estimated tax payment

A **quarterly estimated tax payment** is made in anticipation of the tax that is figured on *Form 1040* Individual Tax Return for that year. A quarterly estimated tax payment can include both income tax and self-employment tax.

See 4.22 Reviewing Types of Taxes

R

rapport

Rapport describes how you and your client connect at some level that enables you to open a continual line of two-way communication. It is synonymous with chemistry. It is one of the components of an effective client-architect relationship.

See 2.23 Defining the Effective Client and Architect Relationship

reciprocate

To **reciprocate** is to be willing to adopt a give-and-take attitude, looking for opportunities for exchanges between you and your clients that may be outside the strict terms of your agreement. It is one of the tactics described to win over clients in the eight **-ates** to conciliate.

See 2.22 Retaining Clients

reciprocation

In an effective client-architect relationship, **reciprocation** refers to the promise you and your client make to each other to do something in exchange for something in return. Reciprocation refers to your contract with each other.

See 2.23 Defining the Effective Client-Architect Relationship

referent power

Referent power comes from the way other people identify with you. Referent power is one of the three sources of *personal power*, which is one of the two forms of a principal's power, along with *position power*.

See 2.3 Using Your Power to Influence

reimbursables

Reimbursables refers to expenses incurred on a particular project. Examples are long-distance telephone calls, blueprinting and photocopying costs, and postage.

See 4.14 Telephone Accounting Codes

relate

To **relate** is to be aware of similarities between you and your clients and to look for opportunities to remark on and revel in them. It is one of the tactics described to win over clients in the eight -**ates** to conciliate.

See 2.22 Retaining Clients

reserve

Reserve refers to the fifth heading of the mnemonic device devised to help you select the right clients for your practice: PETER points for picking clients.

See 2.13 Picking Clients

resource allocator

Resource allocator is one of 11 roles in four categories that you play as the principal of your own firm. As a resource allocator, you decide who will get available time, money, and equipment in the day-to-day running of your practice.

See 2.4 Playing Principal

respect

Respect is one of the components of the effective client-architect relationship. You and your client respect each other, you for your client's goals and your client for your abilities.

See 2.23 Defining the Effective Client and Architect Relationship

reward power

Reward power comes from your ability as principal to acknowledge the performance of others. Reward power is one of the three sources of *position power*, which is one of the two forms of a principal's power, along with *personal power*.

See 2.3 Using Your Power to Influence

road map

A **road map** is an action plan. It sets forth the ways in which you will achieve the goals of your practice.

See 1.4 Designing a Road Map

ruminate

To **ruminate** is to be thinking at all times about how you can best serve your clients. It is one of the tactics described to win over clients in the eight -ates to conciliate.

See 2.22 Retaining Clients

S

Schedule C

Attach **Schedule C** to *Form 1040* Individual Tax Return to report profit or loss from your business. Business expenses are listed on this form along with fees and reimbursables.

See 4.20 Tracking Expenses

Schedule SE

Attach **Schedule SE** to *Form 1040* Individual Tax Return to report self-employment tax.

See 4.22 Reviewing Types of Taxes

scheduling success

Scheduling success is the habit of pacing yourself to handle all the roles you take on as an architect practitioner.

See 3.12 Scheduling Success

self-employment tax

Self-employment tax is the payment that you, as a self-employed individual, make to the U.S. government toward Social Security. It is separate from *income tax*.

See 4.22 Reviewing Types of Taxes

series

Here, **series** is one of the eight reasons to take on a project: The project is the first in what may become a series.

See 2.14 Deciding to Take on a Project

service

Besides making up a large component of what you provide your clients as an architect, **service** refers to one of the eight reasons to take on a project: The project allows you to provide stellar service to a client.

See 2.14 Deciding to Take on a Project

situation analysis guide

A **situation analysis guide** is a strategy that requires you to ask a preordained series of questions to evaluate any situation.

See 1.9 Evaluating Situations

size

Here, **size** refers to one of the eight reasons to take on a project: The project is similar in scale and scope to your other projects or it is small enough to squeeze in or the big one you have been waiting for.

See 2.14 Deciding to Take on a Project

Size A envelope
A **Size A envelope** is the envelope commonly used for small cards, such as an invitation. See *business size envelope*.

See 5.13 Stocking Stationery

slogan
A **slogan** is a catchy phrase that simply characterizes your practice for the public. It is derived from your *thesis sentence*. In *The Architect's Business Problem Solver*, writing a slogan is the second step in defining your firm's image. Writing a thesis sentence is the first step. The third step is designing a *logo*.

See 1.11 Creating an Image for Your Firm

Social Security taxes
Social Security taxes are figured on a portion of wages paid to an employee. As an employer, you match the amount withheld from the employee's wages. See **FICA**.

See 4.22 Reviewing Types of Taxes

socializing
Socializing is the process of helping a new employee fit into your firm.

See 2.36 Socializing a New Employee

sole practitioner
In *The Architect's Business Problem Solver,* a **sole practitioner** is an architect who has no regular employees but who may have consultants.

Sole proprietor
See **sole proprietorship**.

See 4.23 Reporting and Paying Taxes

sole proprietorship

Here, a **sole proprietorship** refers to an architectural practice operated by you alone. The simplest form of business, it makes you singularly responsible for every positive and every negative occurrence related to your practice. In other words, you are your practice. No formal documentation is required to establish a sole proprietorship, other than submitting the appropriate forms at tax time.

See 1.5   Outlining a Business Plan

soul

In *The Architect's Business Problem Solver,* **soul** is the conscience of your practice. The other entities are *heart* and *mind.*

See 1.1   Running Your Firm

sources of power

Sources of power are the different types of personal force you exert to influence others. As the principal in an architectural firm, your power exists in two forms: *position power* and *personal power.* Each of these two forms of power is derived from three sources. Position power comes from *legitimate power, reward power,* and *coercive power.* Personal power comes from *referent power, information power,* and *expert power.*

See 2.3   Using Your Power to Influence

spokesperson

Spokesperson is one of 11 roles in four categories that you play as the principal of your own firm. As a spokesperson, you share information with the outside world that you collect in you role as monitor and believe to be useful in your role as *liaison.*

See 2.4   Playing Principal

standardized forms

Standardized forms are fill-in-the-blank forms that you make up to record information pertaining to activities that recur in your practice, such as meetings, telephone conversations, and ordering stationery. Sample standardized forms are provided for your use in Appendix C.

See 5.13 Stocking Stationery
See 5.14 Using Standardized Forms
See Appendix C: Standardized Forms

startup money

Startup money is the funding you use to open your architectural practice. With it, you would put a security deposit on a rented office and pay the rent and utilities until you start earning fees. Typically, startup money comes from your personal savings, since banks are reluctant to lend money to new businesses.

See 4.4   Finding Startup Money

startup money checklist

A **startup money checklist** is used to determine the costs associated with launching a practice.

See 4.1   Launching a Practice
See 4.4   Finding Startup Money
See 5.13 Stocking Stationery
See 5.14 Using Standardized Forms
See C.12 Startup Money Checklist Form

state unemployment taxes

See unemployment tax.

See 4.22 Reviewing Types of Taxes

state withholdings

State withholdings are the *income tax* that is withheld from an employee's paycheck.

See 4.22 Reviewing Types of Taxes

statement of services rendered

A **statement of services rendered** is the invoice you send to clients for work you have done on their project.

See 4.9 Getting Clients to Pay

stationery and drafting supplies order form

A **stationery and drafting supplies order form** is a *standardized form* used to jot down items before making a telephone call to a mail-order catalog.

See 5.13 Stocking Stationery
See 5.14 Using Standardized Forms
See C.18 Stationery and Drafting Supplies Order Record Form

T

teacher

Teacher is one of the characteristics of the right accountant for your firm.

See 2.45 Hiring an Accountant

telephone accounting codes

Telephone accounting codes are an aspect of a feature offered by telephone service providers that allows you to enter a numeric code to identify the reason for a telephone call or to assign it to a particular project.

See 4.14 Signing Up for Telephone Accounting Codes

telephone call log form

A **telephone call log form** is a *standardized form* on which you keep track of outgoing telephone calls so that you can charge long-distance calls to projects. It comes in handy when you are not a subscriber to telephone service that offers accounting codes as a feature.

See 4.14 Signing Up for Telephone Accounting Codes
See 5.13 Stocking Stationery

See 5.14 Using Standardized Forms
See C.6 Telephone Call Log Form

telephone conversation record form

A **telephone conversation record form** is a *standardized form* on which you jot down notes during a telephone conversation. Better than lined paper, it prompts you for critical information about the party called, time and date of the call, etc.

See 5.13 Stocking Stationery
See 5.14 Using Standardized Forms
See C.7 Telephone Conversation Record Form

telephone message form

A **telephone message form** is a *standardized form* used to record telephone messages left on your answering machine or voice mail as well as messages that you leave on others' answering machines or *voice mail.*

See C.8 Telephone Message Form

terms of employment

The **terms of employment** are *job performance standards.*

See 2.43 Firing an Employee

thank-you note

In the underlying etiquette prescribed in *The Architect's Business Problem Solver,* sending a **thank-you note** is recommended after an initial meeting with a prospective client.

See 2.27 Maintaining Momentum

thesis sentence

In *The Architect's Business Problem Solver,* the term **thesis sentence** is significant in two ways. First, writing a **thesis sentence** is the first step in defining your firm's *image.* It defines your uniqueness and describes how you will demonstrate it in your practice. The second step is writing a *slogan.* The third step is designing a *logo.* Second a **thesis sentence** is the first thing you write in one of the four methods offered in this book to overcome writer's block .

See 2.2 Overcoming Writer's Block
See 1.11 Creating an Image for Your Firm

time

Besides being the topic for Section 3 of this book, **time** is one of the three aspects of client objections when clients take issue with the time it takes for you to render your services.

See 2.19 Fielding Client Objections

time management

Time management refers to how you plan and use time. It is the topic of Section 3: Time of this book.

See Section 3: Time

time-quotient self-report

A **time-quotient self-report** is a method to determine whether or not you are in control of your time.

See 3.8 Evaluating Your Use of Time

time-use flowchart

A time-use flowchart is a visual record of how you use your time.

See 3.9 Planning Time

timing

The byword **timing** is significant in two ways. First, timing is the third heading of the mnemonic device devised to help you select the right clients for your practice: PETER points for picking clients. Second, timing refers to one of the eight reasons to take on a project: The project has a schedule that fits in nicely with your other projects.

See 2.13 Picking Clients
See 2.14 Deciding to Take on a Project

transmittal

A **transmittal**, also known as a **letter of transmittal**, is a written document that announces and accompanies materials such as drawings, specifications, legal documents, product samples, etc. that are being mailed or delivered. A transmittal can be either in the form of a letter that you compose to serve the particular purpose or in the form of a *standardized form* with blanks that you fill in either by hand or on your computer.

See 2.2 Overcoming Writer's Block

U

unemployment tax

Unemployment tax is paid to state and federal governments on a portion of each of your employee's wages to support unemployment programs.

See 4.22 Reviewing Types of Taxes

uniqueness

Uniqueness is the quality that sets you and your practice apart from competitors. It helps to determine the *image* of your firm.

See 1.11 Creating an Image for Your Firm

V

versatile

Versatile is one of the attributes of the right accounting firm for your practice.

See 2.45 Hiring an Accountant

visibility

Visibility is the last of eight reasons to take on a project: The project may gain you recognition.

See 2.14 Deciding to Take on a Project

visitor

Visitor is one of the characteristics of the right accountant for your firm.

See 2.45 Hiring an Accountant

voice mail

Voice mail is a feature offered by some local telephone companies that takes the place of an answering machine in your office. An added feature allows calls to be answered when you are on the line with another party. A disadvantage is that you cannot "screen" or listen in on callers while they are leaving their messages.

See 3.2   Handling Telephone Calls
See 3.3   Playing Telephone Tag
See 4.16 Paying for Voice Mail

W

W-2 Form

A **W-2 Form** reports an employee's yearly wages. As an employer, you distribute W-2 Forms for your employees to attach to their *Form 1040*s.

See 4.22 Reviewing Types of Taxes

withholdings allowance

On a W-2 Form, **withholdings allowances** are based on an individual's particular situation to determine the amount of tax to be taken from that employee's wages.

See 4.22 Reviewing Types of Taxes

writer's block

Writer's block is the inability to begin or continue any writing assignment at hand, which can lead to procrastination of important tasks.

See 2.2 Overcoming Writer's block

APPENDIX

List of Mnemonic Devices and Step-by-Step Solutions

SECTION 1: BUILDING BLOCKS

The Three Human Entities of Your Practice

See 1.1 Running Your Firm

Ten Steps to a Mission Statement

See 1.2 Writing a Mission Statement

Three R's of Roadmapping

See 1.4 Designing a Road Map

Five Steps to Success

See 1.6 Strategizing for Success

Four Steps to a Marketing Plan

See 1.8 Developing a Marketing Plan

The Three Components of Your Firm's Image

See 1.11 Creating an Image for Your Firm

SECTION 2: PEOPLE

Fifteen Things That Successful Bosses Do

See 2.1 Evaluating Yourself as a Boss

Four Methods for Overcoming Writer's Block

See 2.2 Overcoming Writer's Block

The Two Forms of a Principal's Power

See 2.3 Using Your Power to Influence

Eleven Roles to Play as Principal

See 2.4 Playing Principal

Four Roles to Play as Manager

See 2.5 Playing Manager

Two Part Formula for Writing a Press Release

See 2.7 Writing a Press Release

A Dozen Ways to Get Noticed

See 2.11 Getting Noticed

PETER Points for Picking Clients

See 2.13 Picking Clients

Eight Reasons to Take on a Project

See 2.14 Deciding to Take on a Project

Six Sections in a Typical Proposal to Clients

See 2.15 Writing a Proposal

RPMs Toward an Agreement

See 2.17 Getting to an Agreement

Three Aspects of Client Objections

See 2.19 Fielding Client Objections

Eight -ates to Conciliate

See 2.22 Retaining Clients

The 3 R's of an Effective Client and Architect Relationship

See 2.23 Defining the Effective Client and Architect Relationship

Two Attributes of a Good Listener

See 2.25 Honing Listening Skills

SECTION 3: TIME

Three Lists for Avoiding Repeated Mistakes
See 3.1 Avoiding Repeated Mistakes

Four Ways to Manage Telephone Calls
See 3.2 Handling Telephone Calls

Four Ways to Spend Less in Line at the Post Office
See 3.4 Cutting Down Time at the Post Office

Four Courses of a Master To-Do List
See 3.5 Keeping a Master To-Do List

Keeping Your Master To-Do List Current
See 3.6 Updating a Master To-Do List

Four Steps to Keeping a Daily To-Do List
See 3.7 Making a Daily To-Do List

Ten Signs that You are in Control of Your Time
See 3.8 Evaluating Your Use of Time

Seven Steps for Keeping Meetings on Time and on Track
See 3.10 Keeping Meetings on Time

Ten Tips for Scheduling Success
See 3.12 Scheduling Success

A Dozen Signs of an Organized Individual
See 3.14 Getting Organized

SECTION 4: MONEY

Ten Tips for Borrowing Money
See 4.5 Borrowing Money

Five Steps in Building Relationship with a Banker
See 4.6 Getting a Business Loan

SECTION 5: STUFF

Bibliography

Bliss, Edwin C. 1984. *Doing It Now*. New York: Bantam Books.

Bliss, Edwin C. 1978. *Getting Things Done: The ABC's of Time Management*. New York: Bantam Books.

Clark, Scott A. 1991. *Beating the Odds*. New York: AMACOM.

Covey, Stephen R., A. Roger Merrill, and Rebecca R. Merrill. 1994. *First Things First*. New York: Simon & Schuster.

Crosby, Philip B. 1981. *The Art of Getting Your Own Sweet Way*. New York: McGraw-Hill.

Cuff, Dana. 1991. *Architecture: The Story of Practice*. Cambridge, Mass.: MIT Press.

Deep, Sam, and Lyle Sussman. 1990. *Smart Moves*. Reading, Mass.: Addison-Wesley.

Dixon, Robert L. 1982. *The McGraw-Hill 36-Hour Accounting Course*. New York: McGraw-Hill.

Emmerling, John. 1991. *It Only Takes One*. New York: Simon & Schuster.

Esperti, Robert A., and Renno L. Peterson. 1984. *Incorporating Your Talents*. New York: McGraw-Hill.

Franklin, James R., FAIA. 1990. *Current Practices in Small Firm Management: An Architect's Notebook*. Washington: American Institute of Architects.

Fritz, Roger. 1987. *Nobody Gets Rich Working for Somebody Else*. New York: Dodd, Mead & Company.

Gill, Michael, and Sheila Paterson. 1996. *Fired Up! From Corporate Kiss-Off to Entrepreneurial Kick-Off*. New York: Viking Penguin.

Haviland, David, ed. 1988. *The Architect's Handbook of Professional Practice,* 11th ed. Washington: American Institute of Architects.

Hedrick, Lucy H. 1992. *365 Ways to Save Time.* New York: Hearst Books.

Hirsch, E. D., Jr., Joseph F. Kett, and James Trefil. 1988. *Dictionary of Cultural Literacy.* Boston: Houghton Mifflin.

Kaderlan, Norman. 1991. *Designing Your Practice.* New York: McGraw-Hill.

Kirk, Stephen J., and Kent F. Spreckelmeyer. 1988. *Creative Design Decisions.* New York: Van Nostrand Reinhold.

Mayer, Jeffrey J. 1990. *If You Haven't Got the Time to Do It Right, When Will You Find the Time to Do It Over?* New York: Simon & Schuster.

Michels, Gloria. 1988. *How to Make Yourself (or Anyone Else) Famous.* New York: Cross Gates Publishing.

Murphy, Kevin J. 1987. *Effective Listening.* New York: Bantam Books.

Peters, Thomas J., and Robert H. Waterman, Jr. 1982. *In Search of Excellence.* New York: Warner Books.

Pressman, Andy. 1995. *The Fountainheadache: The Politics of Architect-Client Relations.* New York: John Wiley & Sons.

Raskin, Patricia J. 1991. *Success, Your Dreams and You.* Malibu, Calif.: Roundtable Publishing.

Rubeling, Albert W., Jr. 1994. *How to Start and Operate Your Own Design Firm.* New York: McGraw-Hill.

Schreiber, Norman. 1990. *Your Home Office.* New York: Harper & Row.

Shenson, Howard L., and Jerry R. Wilson. 1993. *138 Quick Ideas to Get More Clients.* New York: John Wiley & Sons.

Shilling, Dana. 1983. *Be Your Own Boss.* New York: Penguin Books.

Solomon, Muriel. 1990. *Working with Difficult People.* Englewood Cliffs, N.J.: Prentice-Hall.

Stasiowski, Frank A., AIA. 1991. *Staying Small Successfully: A Guide for Architects, Engineers and Design Professionals.* New York: John Wiley & Sons.

Stevens, Mark. 1988. *The Macmillan Small Business Handbook.* New York: Macmillan.

Winston, Stephanie. 1978. *Getting Organized.* New York: W.W. Norton.

Winston, Stephanie. 1983. *The Organized Executive.* New York: Warner Books.

Index

About the Author

KEVIN MASON runs his own residential architecture practice in northern New Jersey, where he specializes in designing period additions to old houses and brings a historian's eye to designing new houses. He offers design counseling services to homeowners in search of ideas and technical advice about projects they are considering.

Before opening his own practice, the author filled the dual roles of director of administration and project director at the architecture firm of Gerald Allen & Associates in New York City. He gained business experience as a consultant for the facilities planning department of John Blair & Company, a television and radio sales representative firm in New York.

The author holds undergraduate and graduate degrees in architecture from Columbia University. Licensed in New Jersey and New York and NCARB certified, the author sits on the Fanwood, New Jersey, Historic Preservation Commission. He is a member of the American Institute of Architects.